DO YOU KNOW

Piranhas?

Written by
Alain M. Bergeron
Michel Quintin
Sampar

Illustrations by
Sampar

Translated by
Pamela Doll

Fitzhenry & Whiteside

First published as "Savais-Tu? Les Piranhas" by Editions Michel Quintin,
Québec, Canada, J0E 2N0

Published in Canada by Fitzhenry & Whiteside, 195 Allstate Parkway,
Markham, Ontario L3R 4T8
Published in the United States by Fitzhenry & Whiteside, 311 Washington Street,
Brighton, Massachusetts 02135

www.fitzhenry.ca godwit@fitzhenry.ca

10 9 8 7 6 5 4 3 2 1

Library and Archives Canada Cataloguing in Publication
Bergeron, Alain M., 1957-
[Piranhas. English]
Do you know piranhas? / written by Alain M. Bergeron, Michel Quintin,
Sampar ; illustrations by Sampar ; translated by Pamela Doll.
Translation of: Les piranhas.
Includes index.
ISBN 978-1-55455-353-2 (paperback)
1. Piranhas--Juvenile literature. 2. Piranhas--Comic books, strips, etc.
3. Graphic novels. I. Quintin, Michel, 1953-, author II. Sampar, author,
illustrator III. Title. IV. Title: Piranhas. English.
QL638.C5B4713 2016 j597'.48 C2015-907522-X

Publisher Cataloging-in-Publication Data (U.S.)
Names: Bergeron, Alain M., 1957-, author. | Quintin, Michel, author. | Sampar, author, illustrator. |Doll, Pamela, translator. Title: Do you know piranhas? / written by Alain M. Bergeron, Michel Quintin, Sampar ; illustrations by Sampar ; translated by Pamela Doll.
Description: Markham, Ontario : Fitzhenry & Whiteside Limited, 2019. | Previously published in French as "Savais-tu les Piranhas?" | Includes index. |Summary: "Fascinating and informative facts about piranhas in a graphic novel format" – Provided by publisher.
Identifiers: ISBN 978-1-55455-353-2 (paperback)
Subjects: LCSH: Piranhas -- Juvenile literature | Piranhas -- Cartoons and comics | Nonfiction comics. | BISAC: JUVENILE NONFICTION / Animals / Fishes.
Classification: LCC QL638.C5B474 |DDC 597.48 – dc23

Fitzhenry & Whiteside acknowledges with thanks the Canada Council for the Arts, and the Ontario Arts Council for their support of our publishing program. We acknowledge the financial support of the Government of Canada through the Canada Book Fund (CBF) for our publishing activities.

ONTARIO ARTS COUNCIL
CONSEIL DES ARTS DE L'ONTARIO
an Ontario government agency
un organisme du gouvernement de l'Ontario

Canada Council for the Arts
Conseil des Arts du Canada

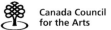

Cover and text design by Cheryl Chen
Cover image by Sampar
Printed in China by Sheck Wah Tong Printing Press Ltd.

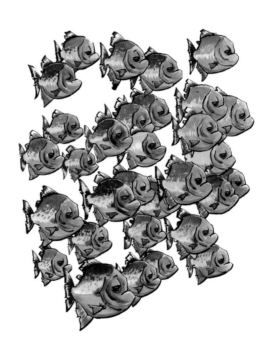

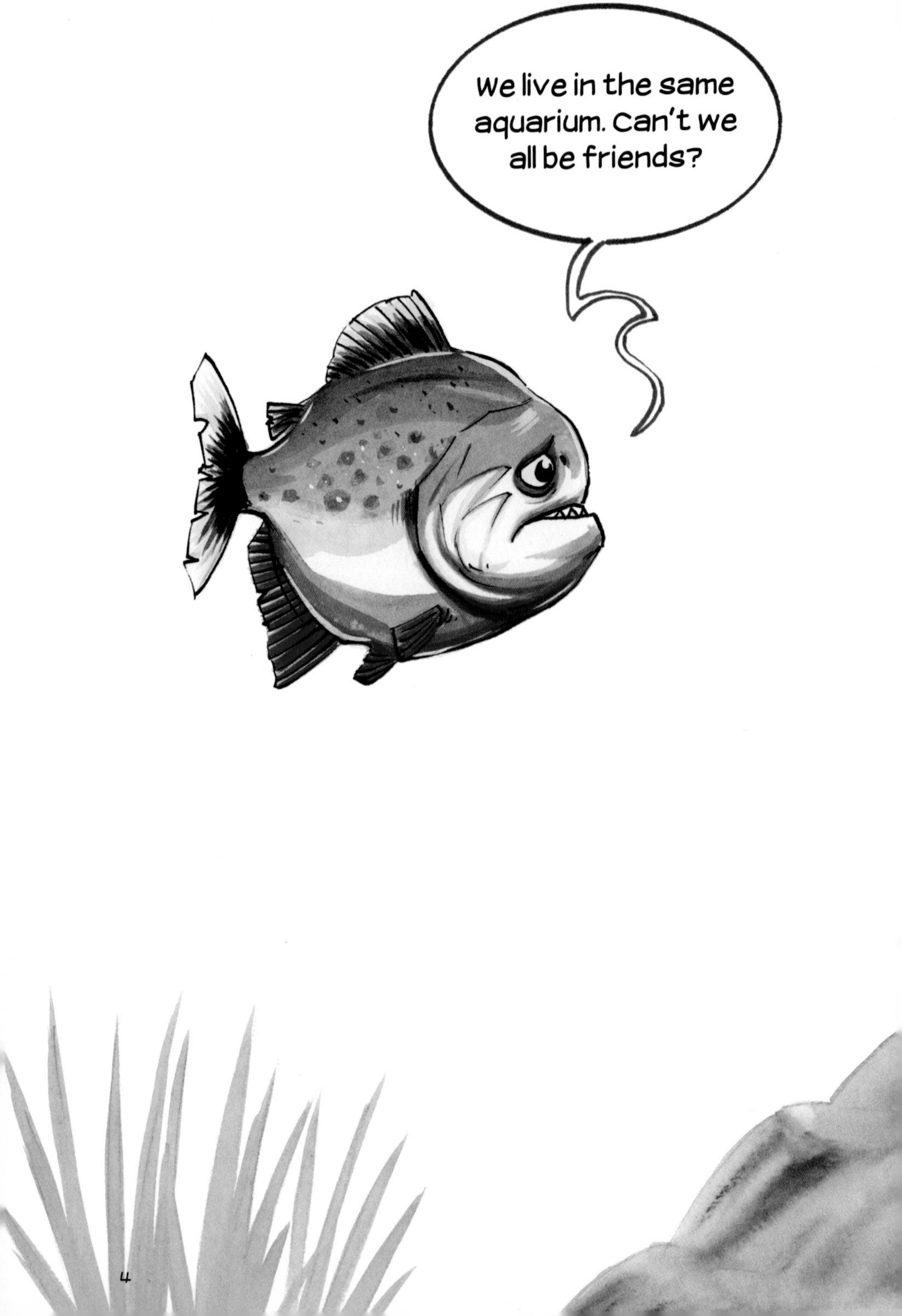
We live in the same aquarium. Can't we all be friends?

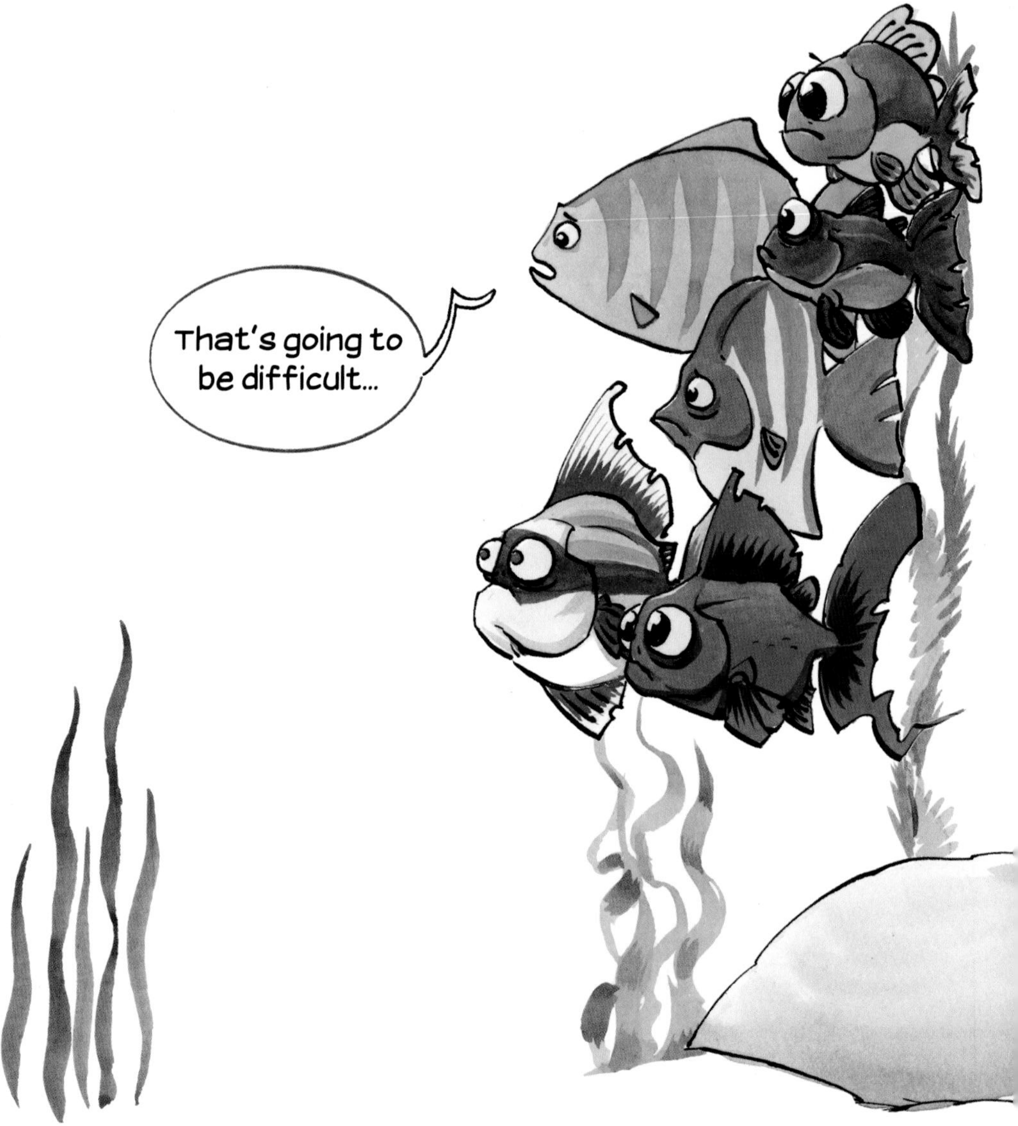
That's going to be difficult...

Piranhas live in **soft water**. They can only be found in South America.

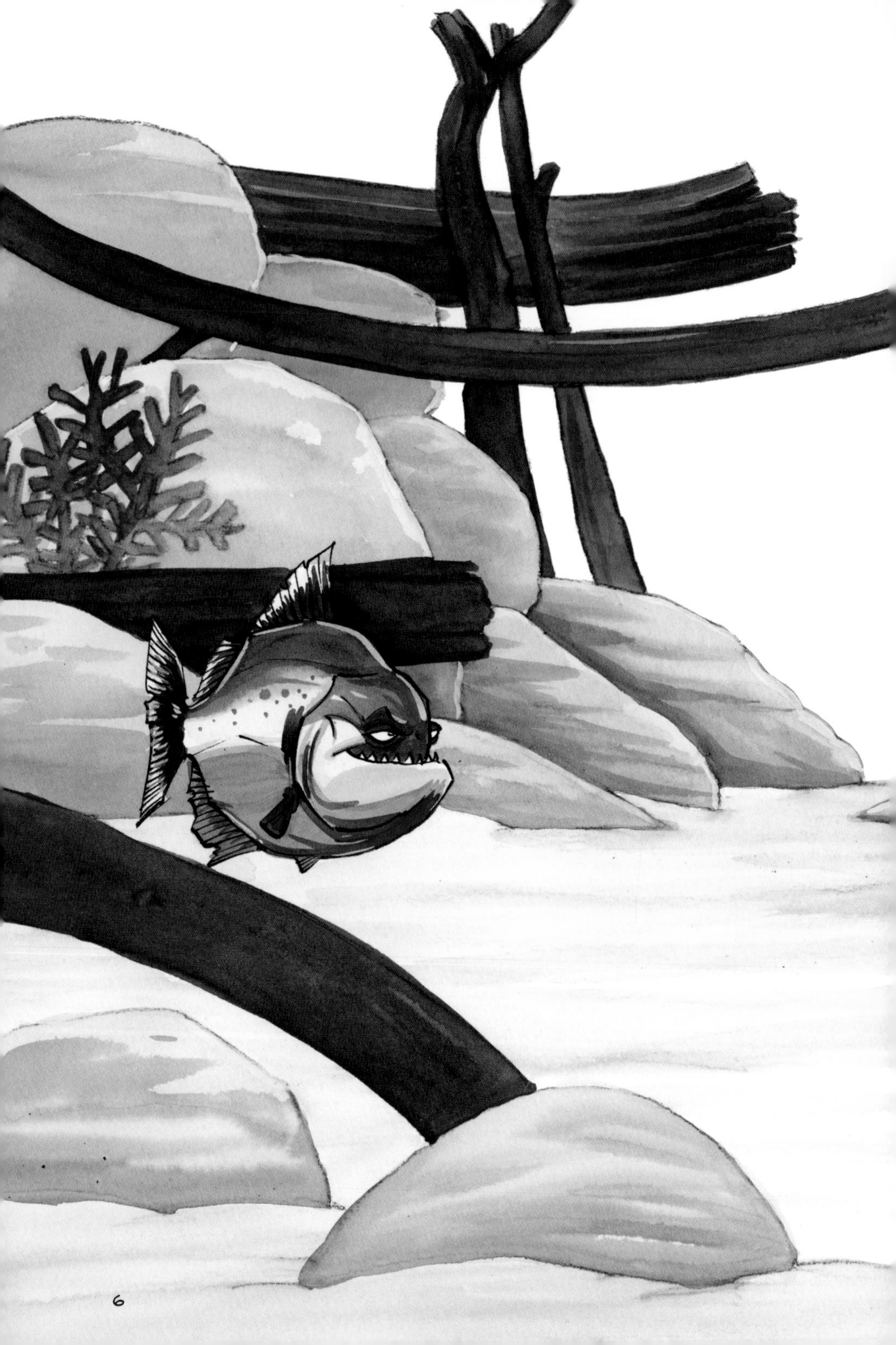

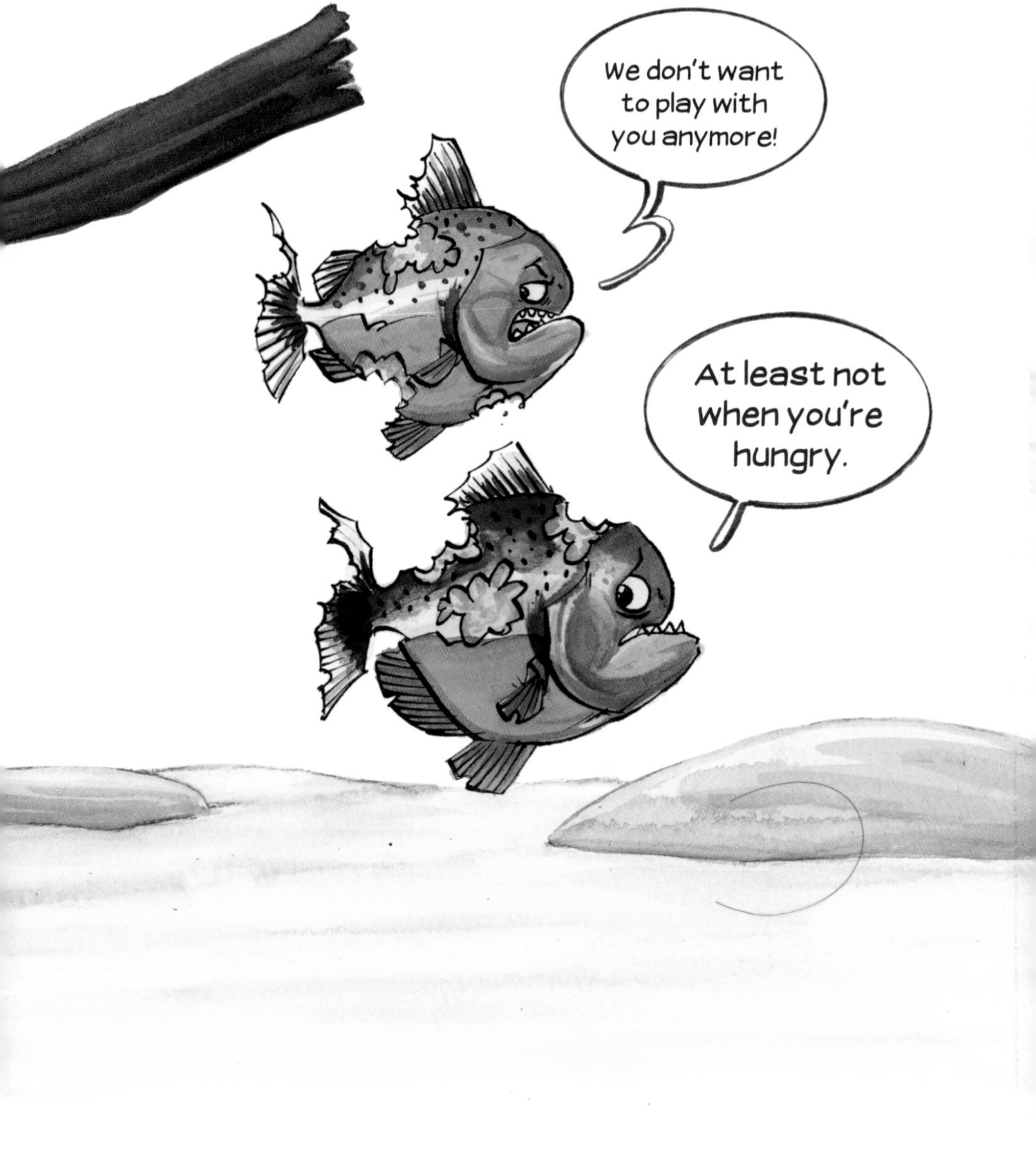
We don't want to play with you anymore!
At least not when you're hungry.

There are approximately 30 **species** of piranhas in the world, but only about 4 species are considered dangerous.

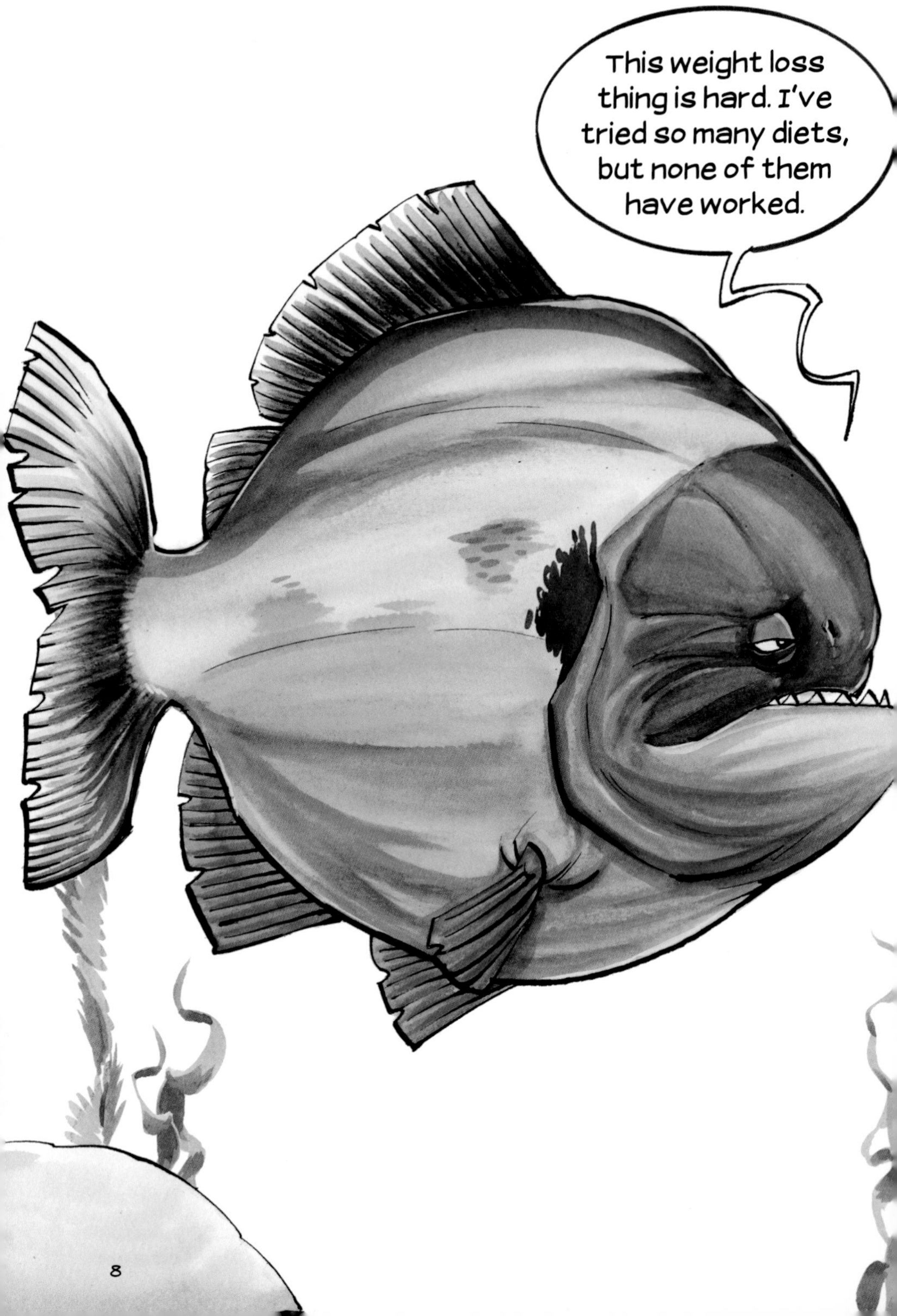
This weight loss thing is hard. I've tried so many diets, but none of them have worked.

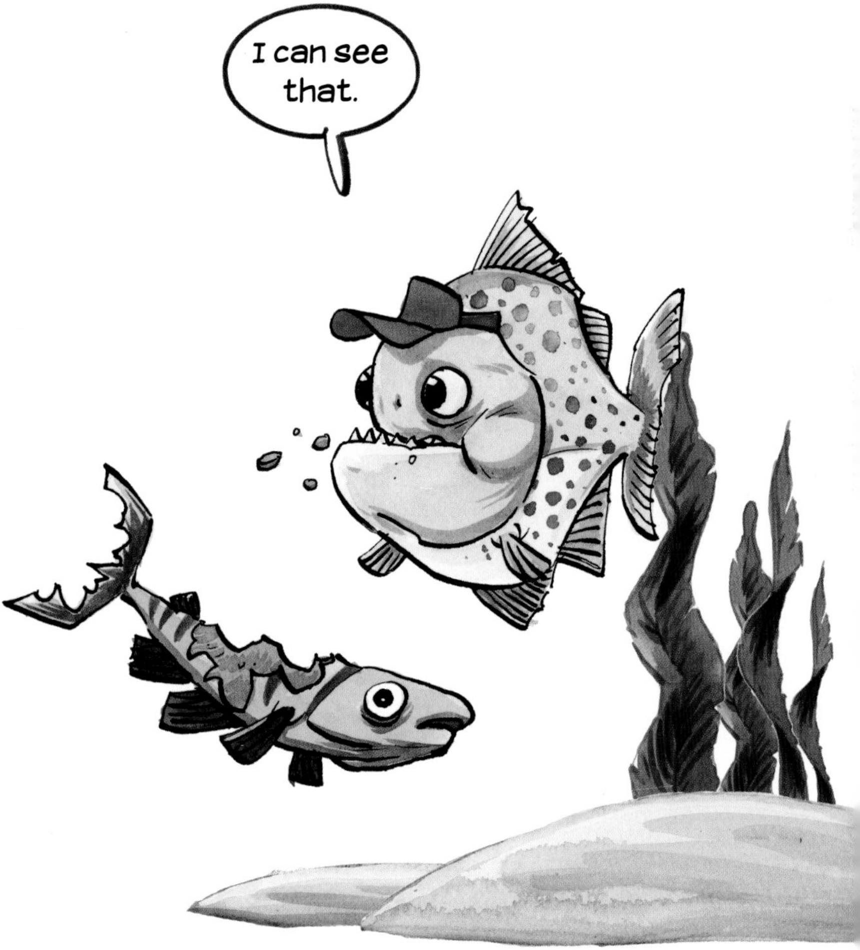
I can see that.

Some of these fish can measure up to 60 centimetres (23.6 inches) in length.

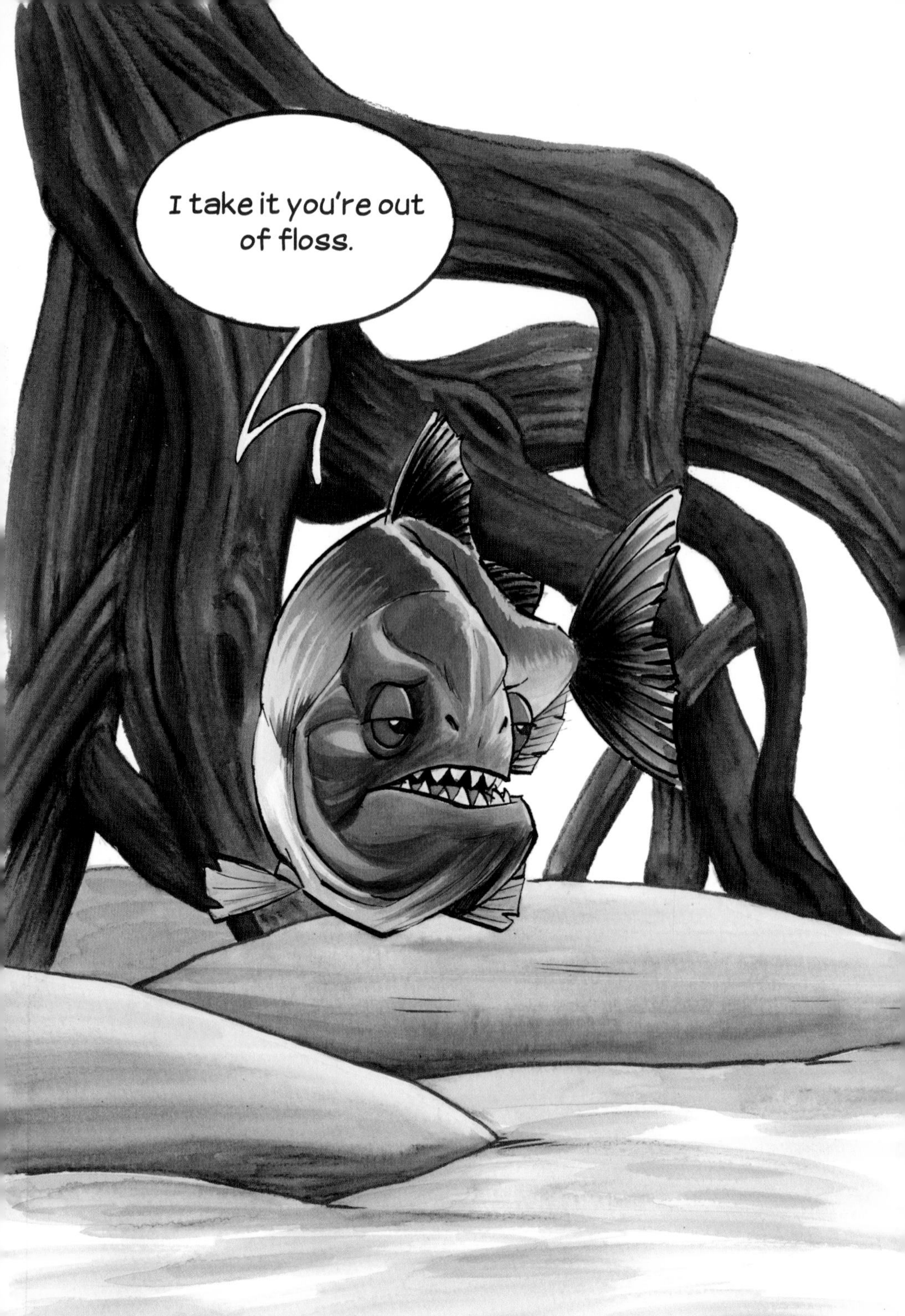
I take it you're out of floss.

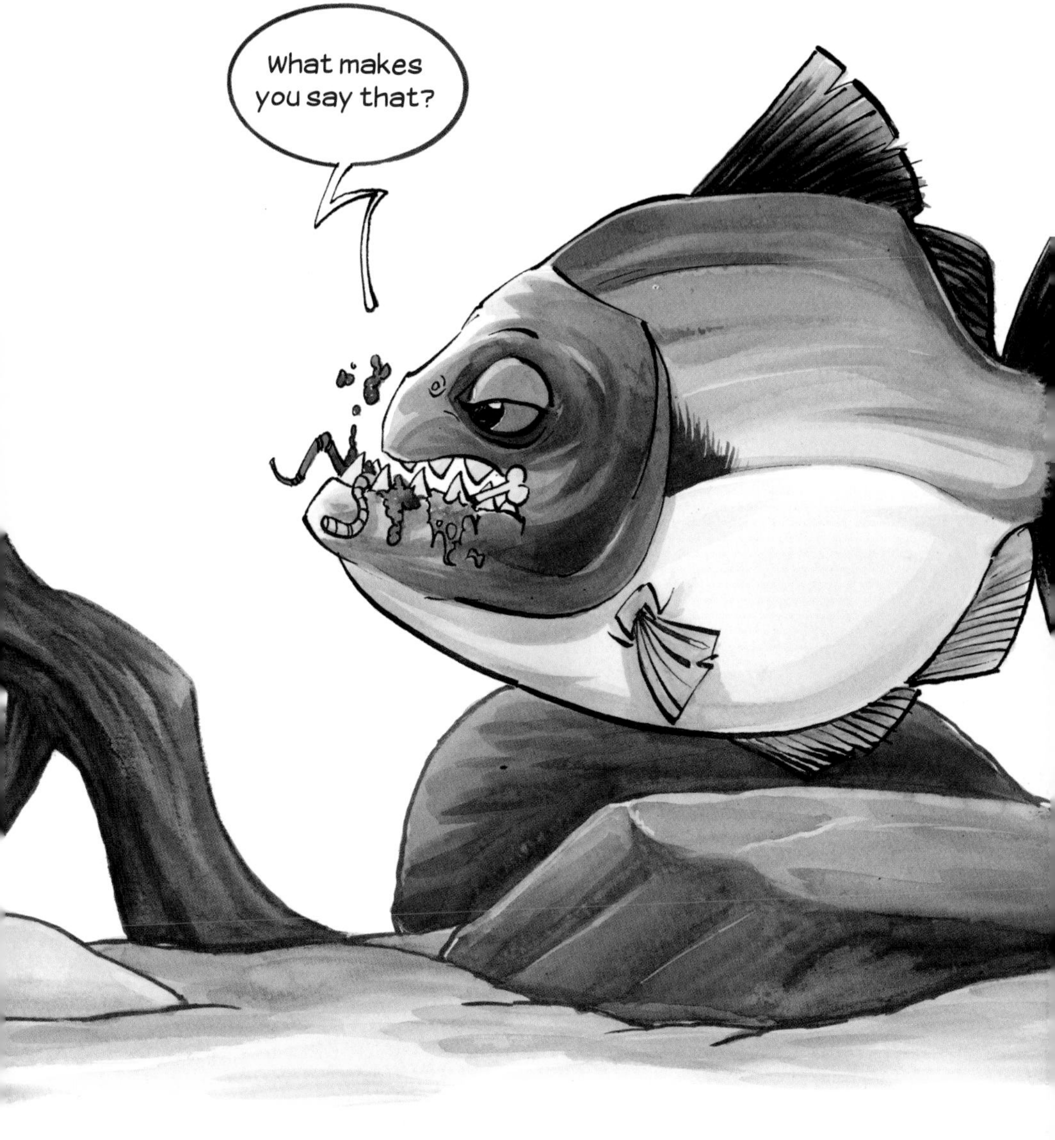
What makes you say that?

A piranha's jaws are extremely powerful and their teeth are as sharp as razor blades.

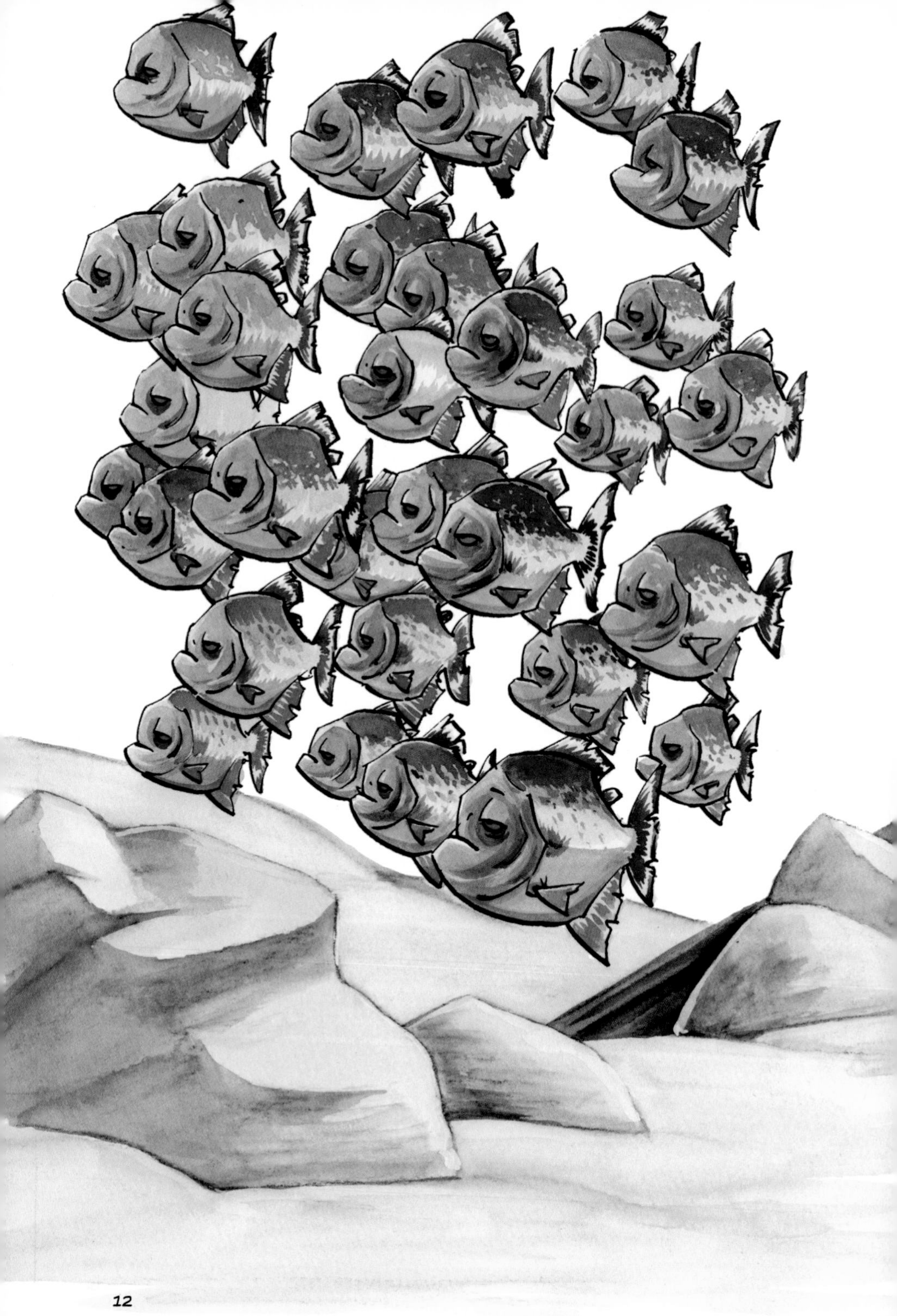

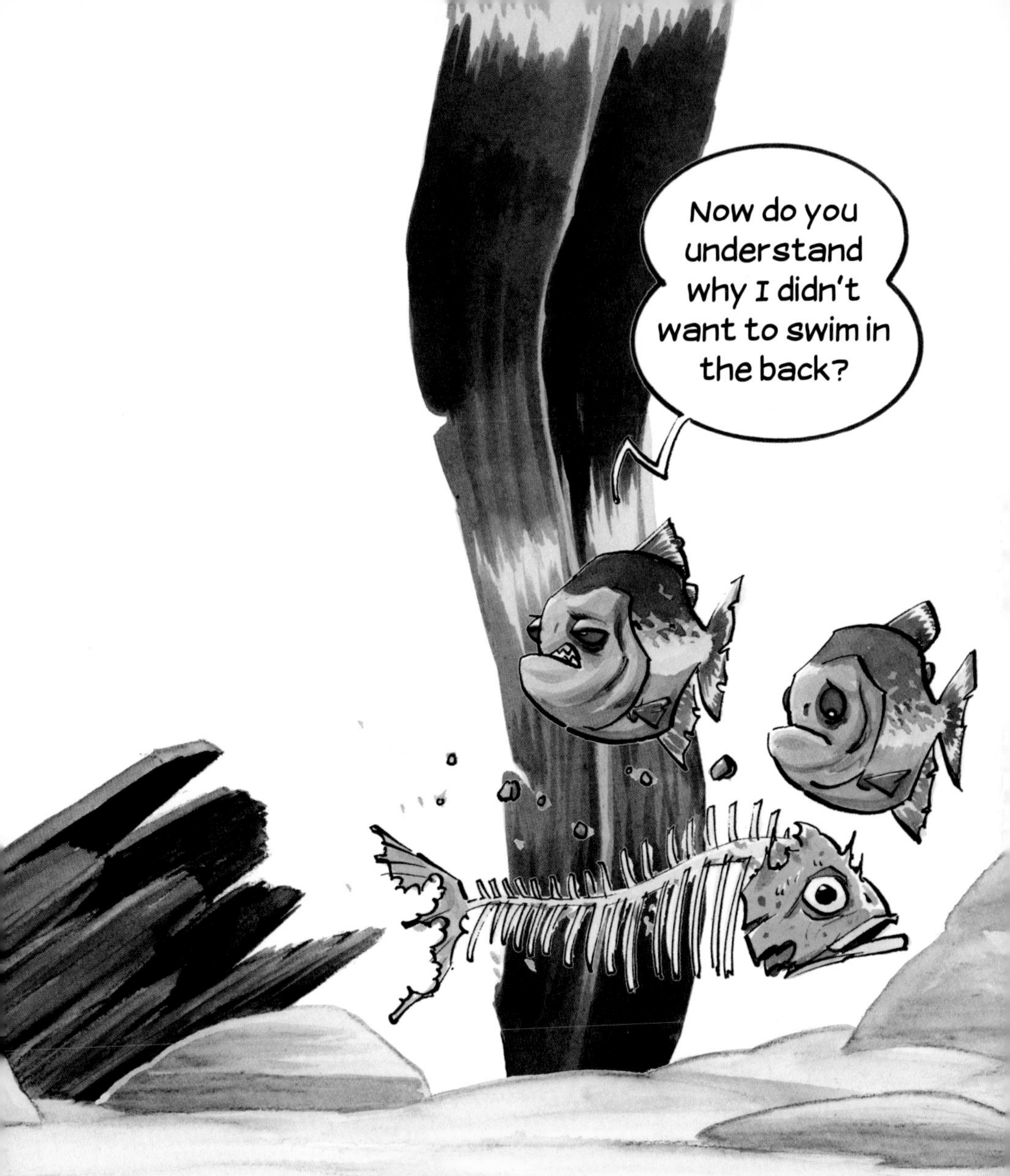
Now do you understand why I didn't want to swim in the back?

The majority of piranha species live in groups. Some **shoals** can consist of several thousand piranhas.

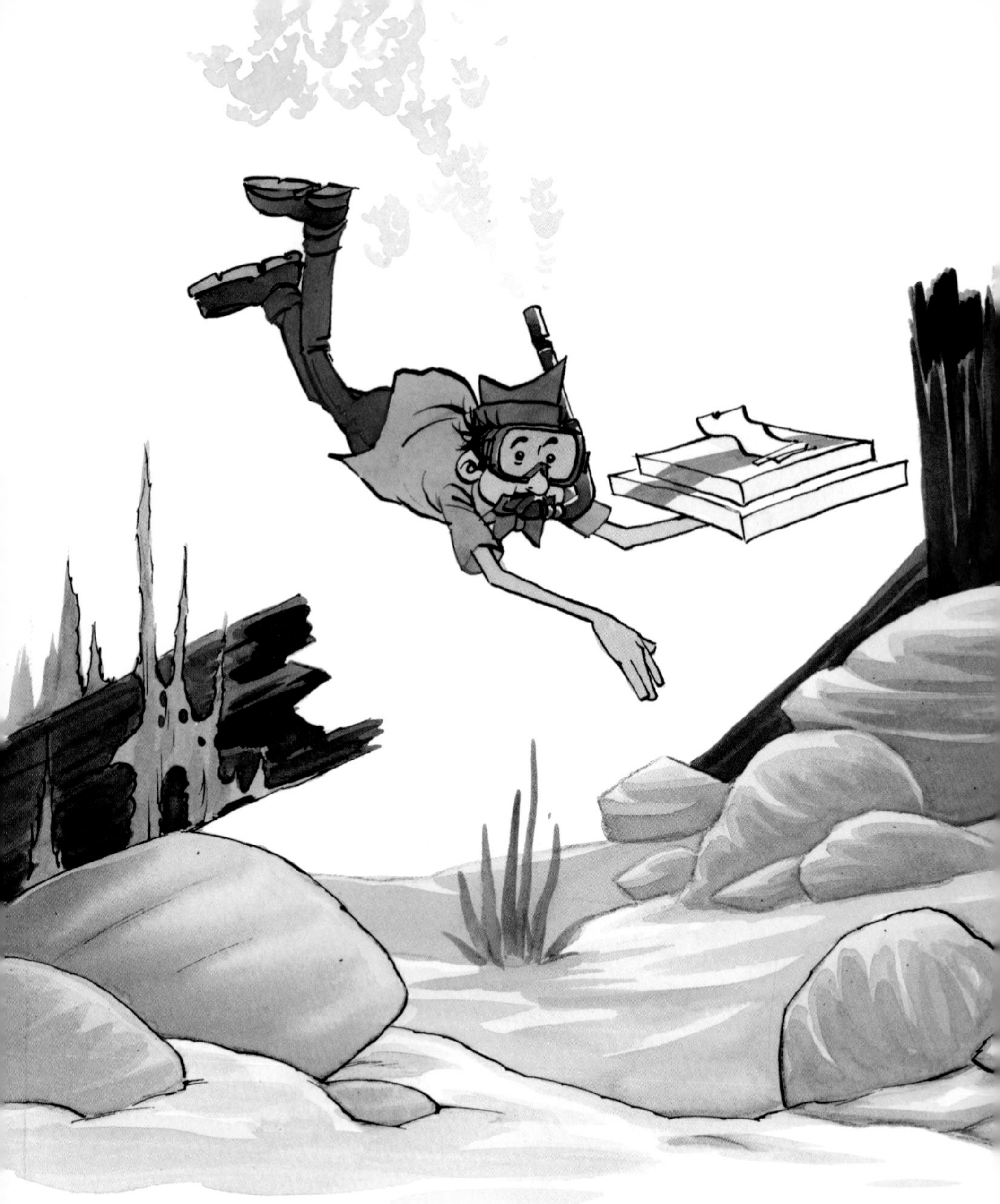

Piranhas' diets vary according to their species, their age, the season, and the food availability.

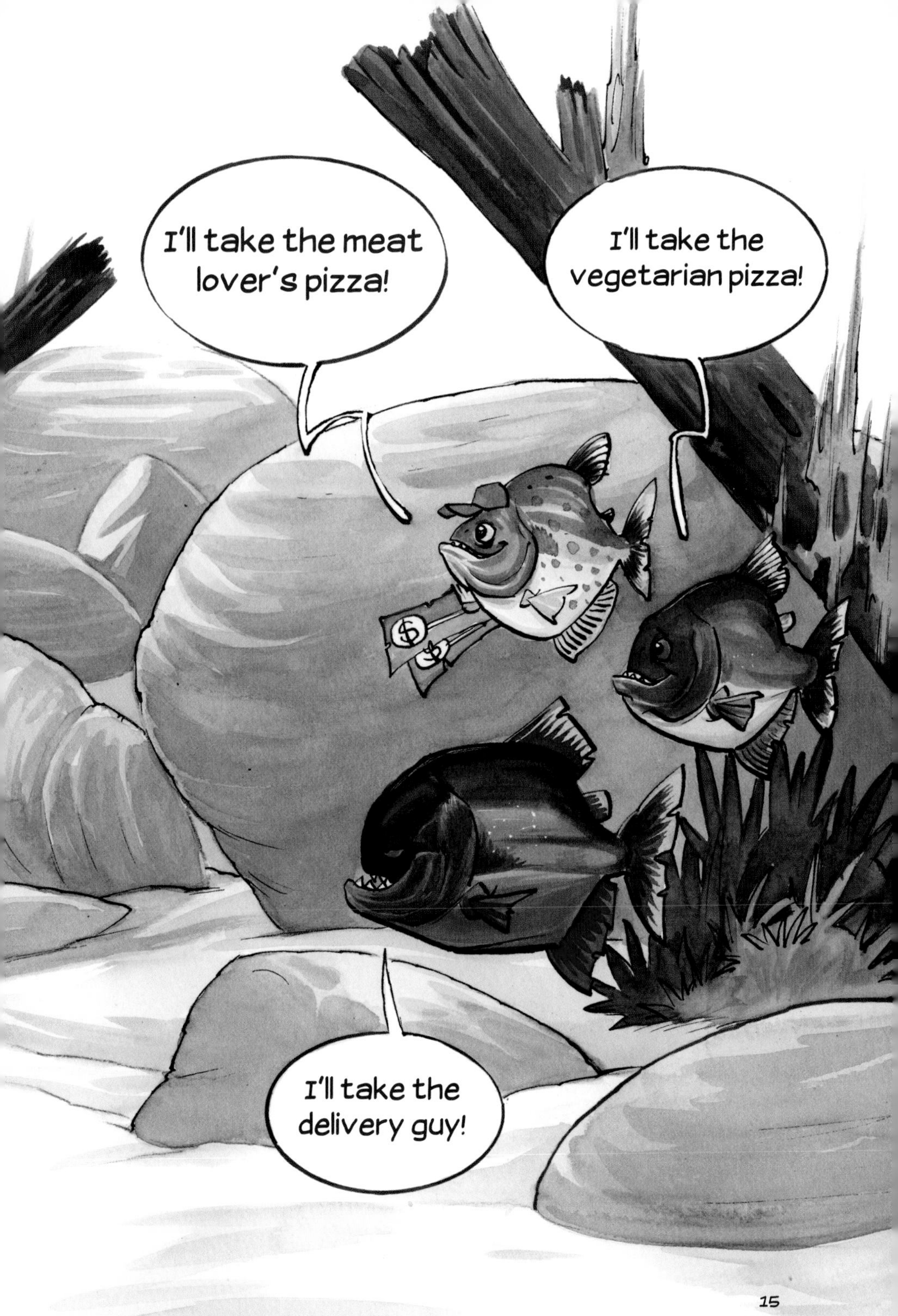
I'll take the meat lover's pizza!
I'll take the vegetarian pizza!
I'll take the delivery guy!

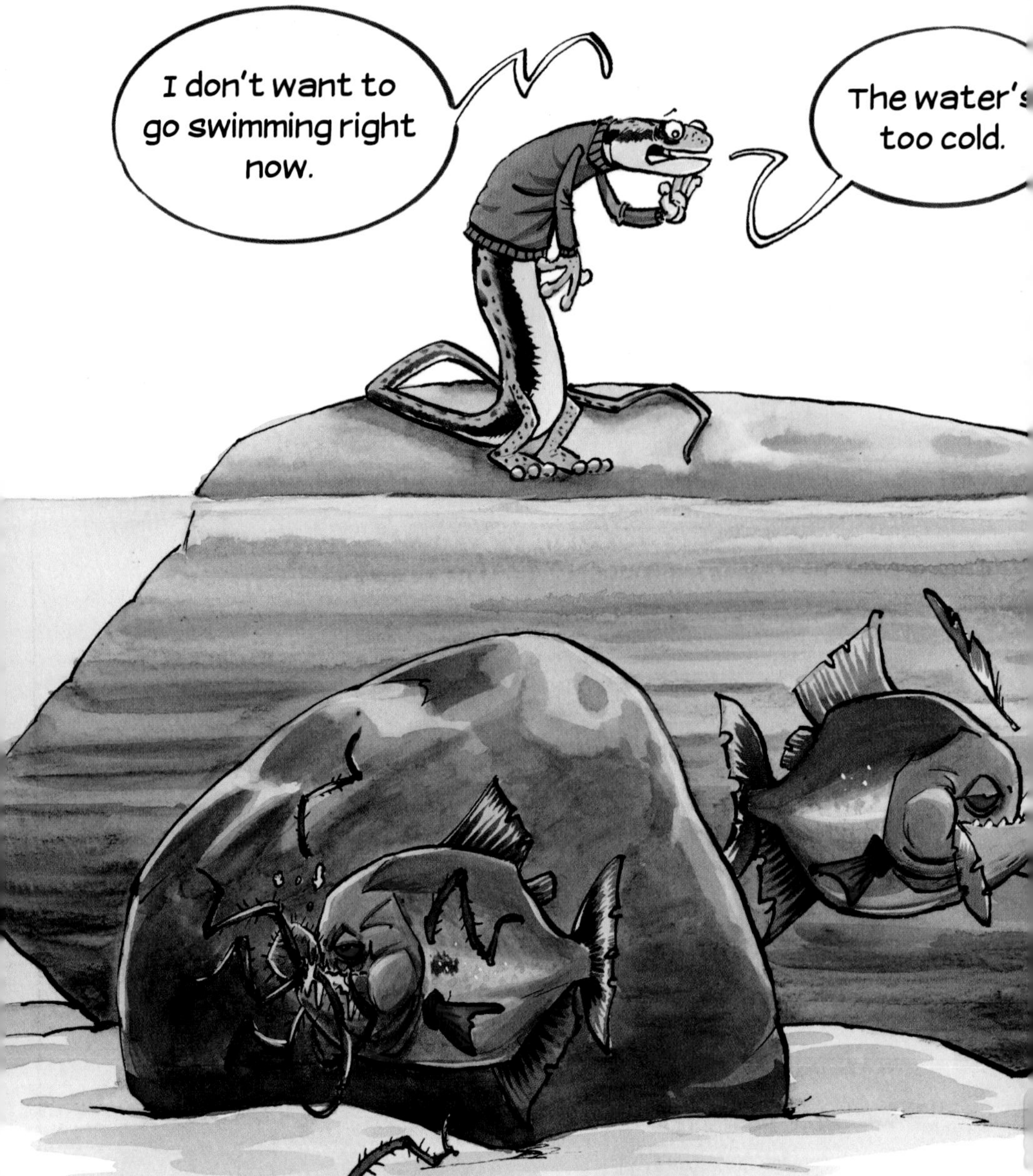
I don't want to go swimming right now.
The water's too cold.

Besides fish, piranhas also eat **mammals**, birds, **reptiles**, and insects.

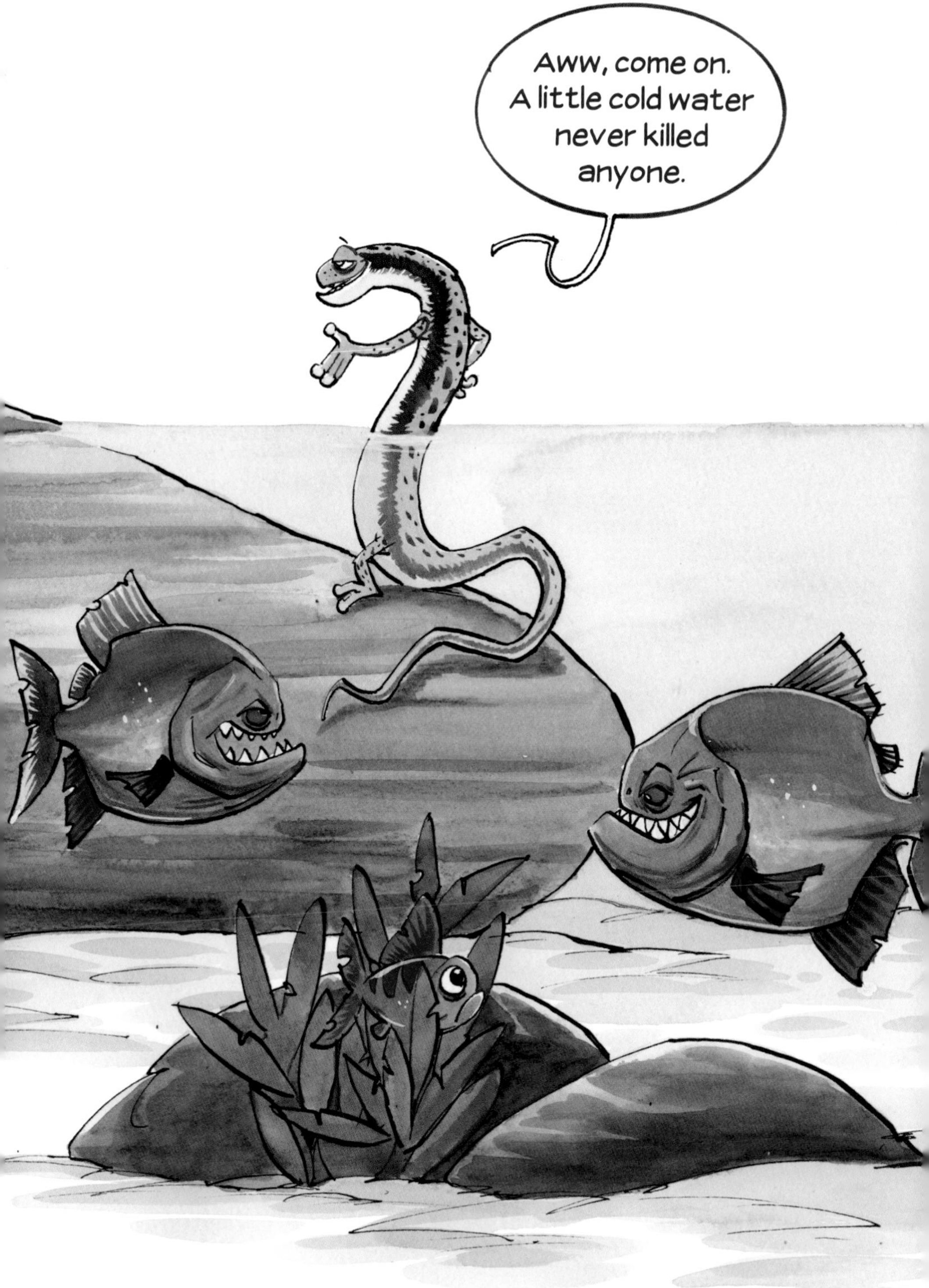
Aww, come on. A little cold water never killed anyone.

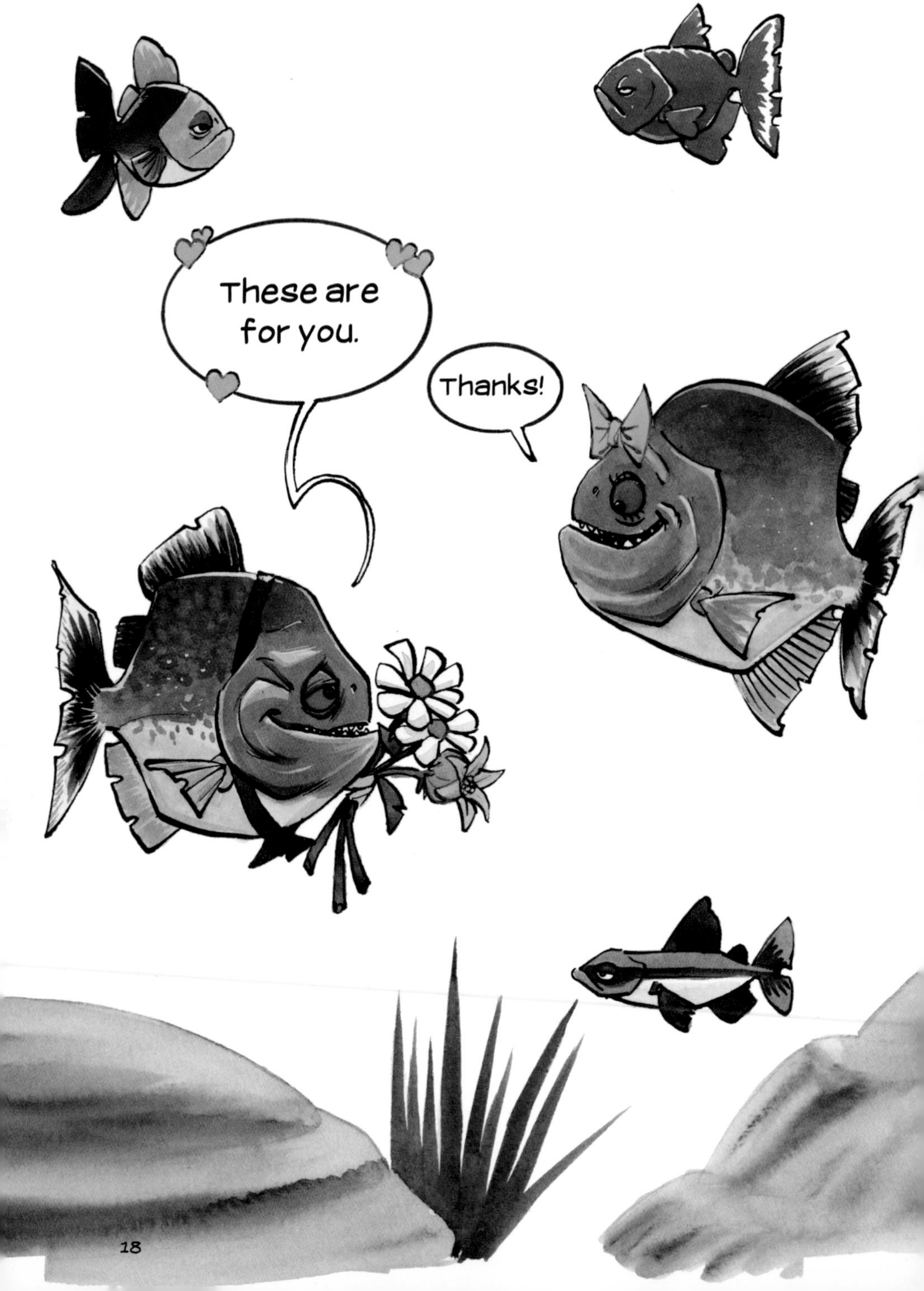
These are for you.
Thanks!

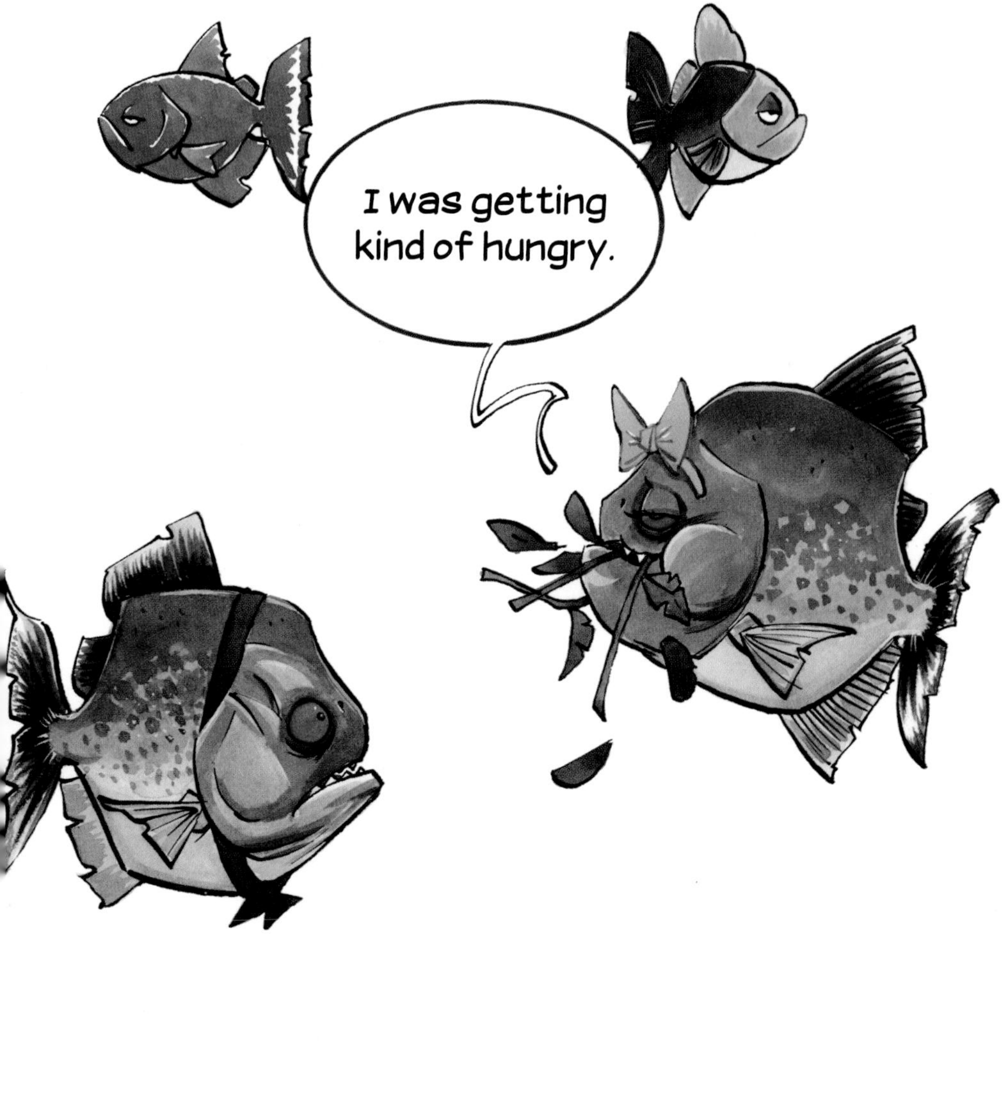
I was getting kind of hungry.

Piranhas also eat vegetation, such as fruits, grains, flowers, and leaves.

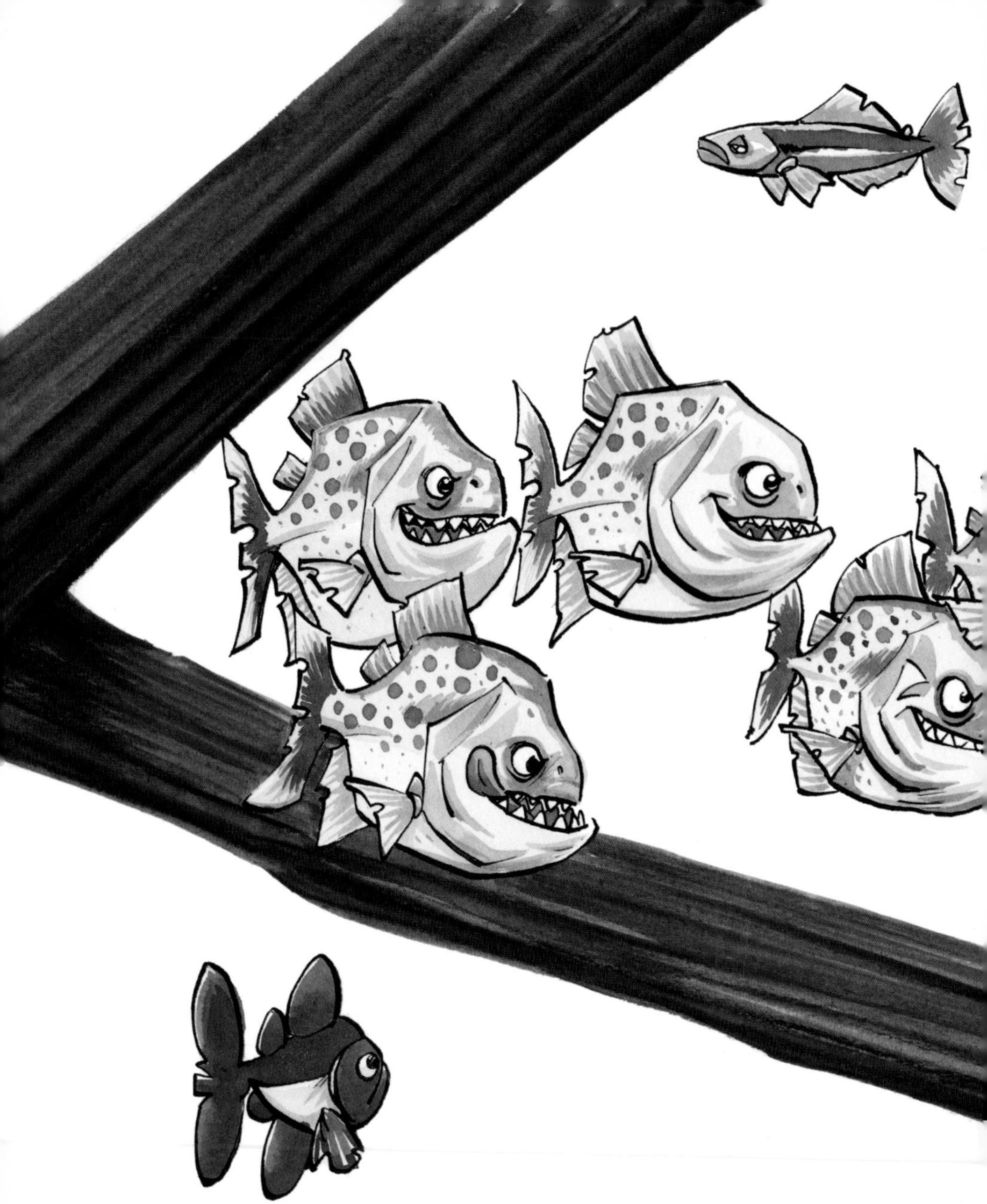

Some species are almost exclusively **vegetarian**.

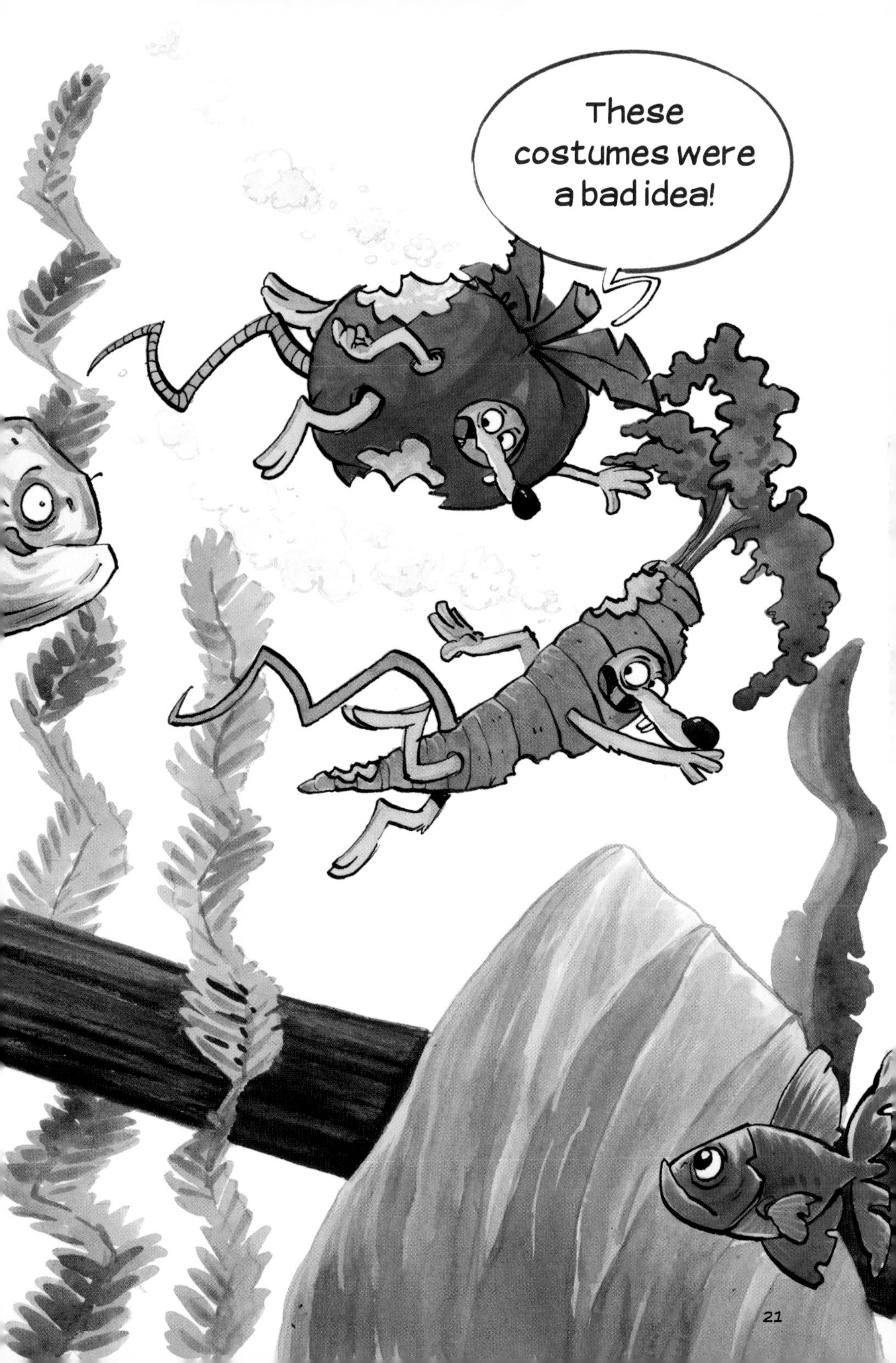
These costumes were a bad idea!

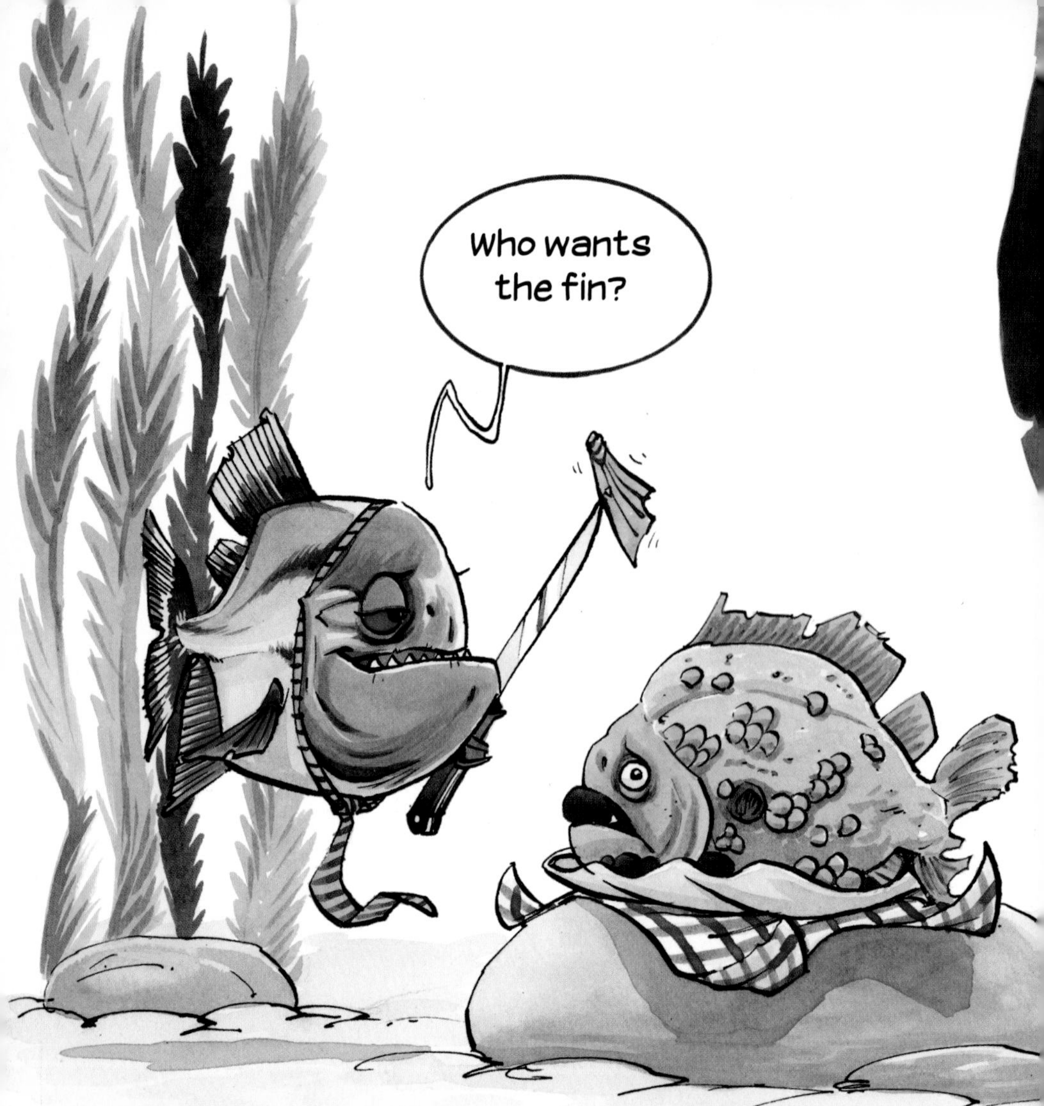
Who wants
the fin?

Some species feed on the scales and fins of other fish.

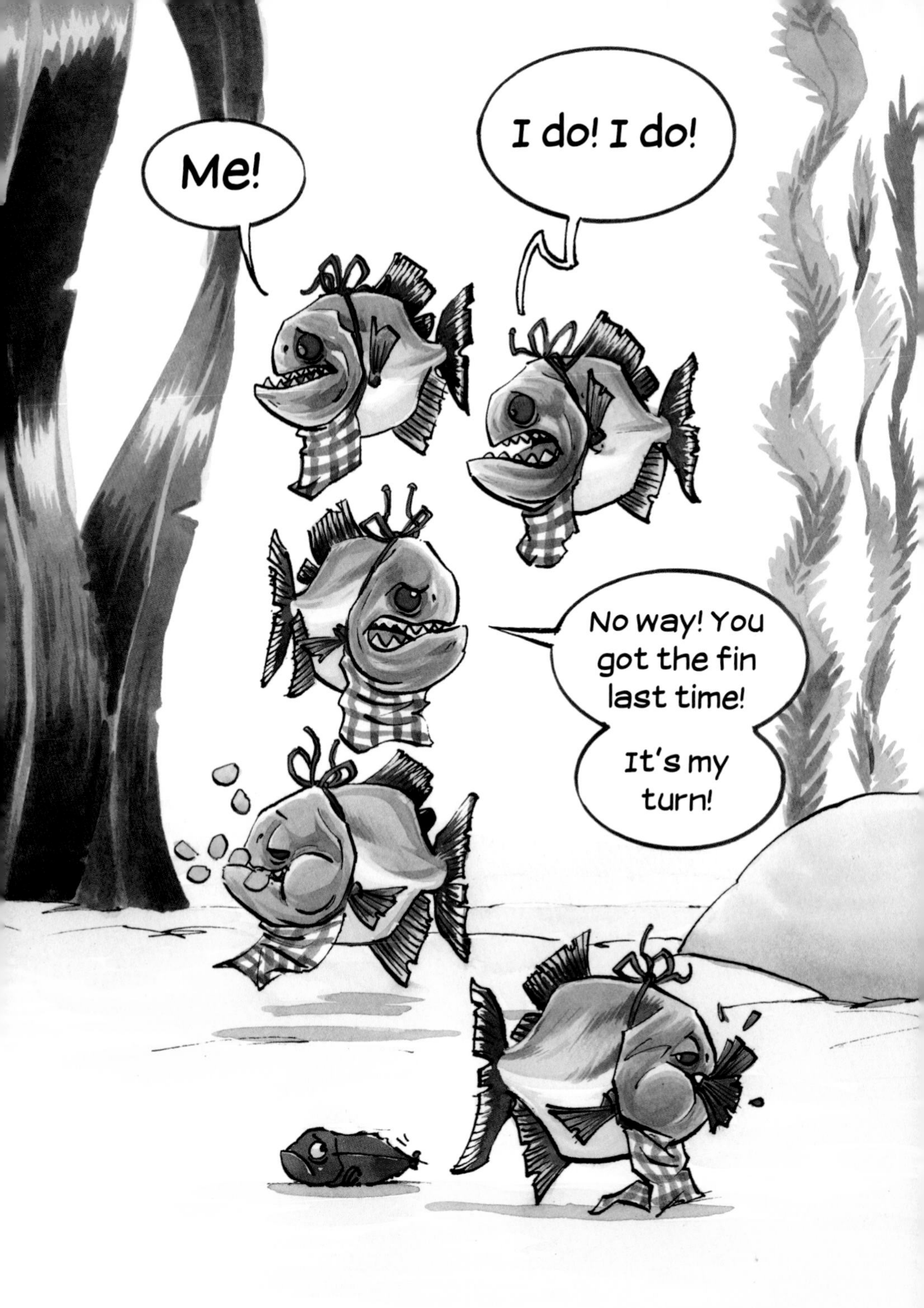
Me!
I do! I do!
No way! You got the fin last time!
It's my turn!

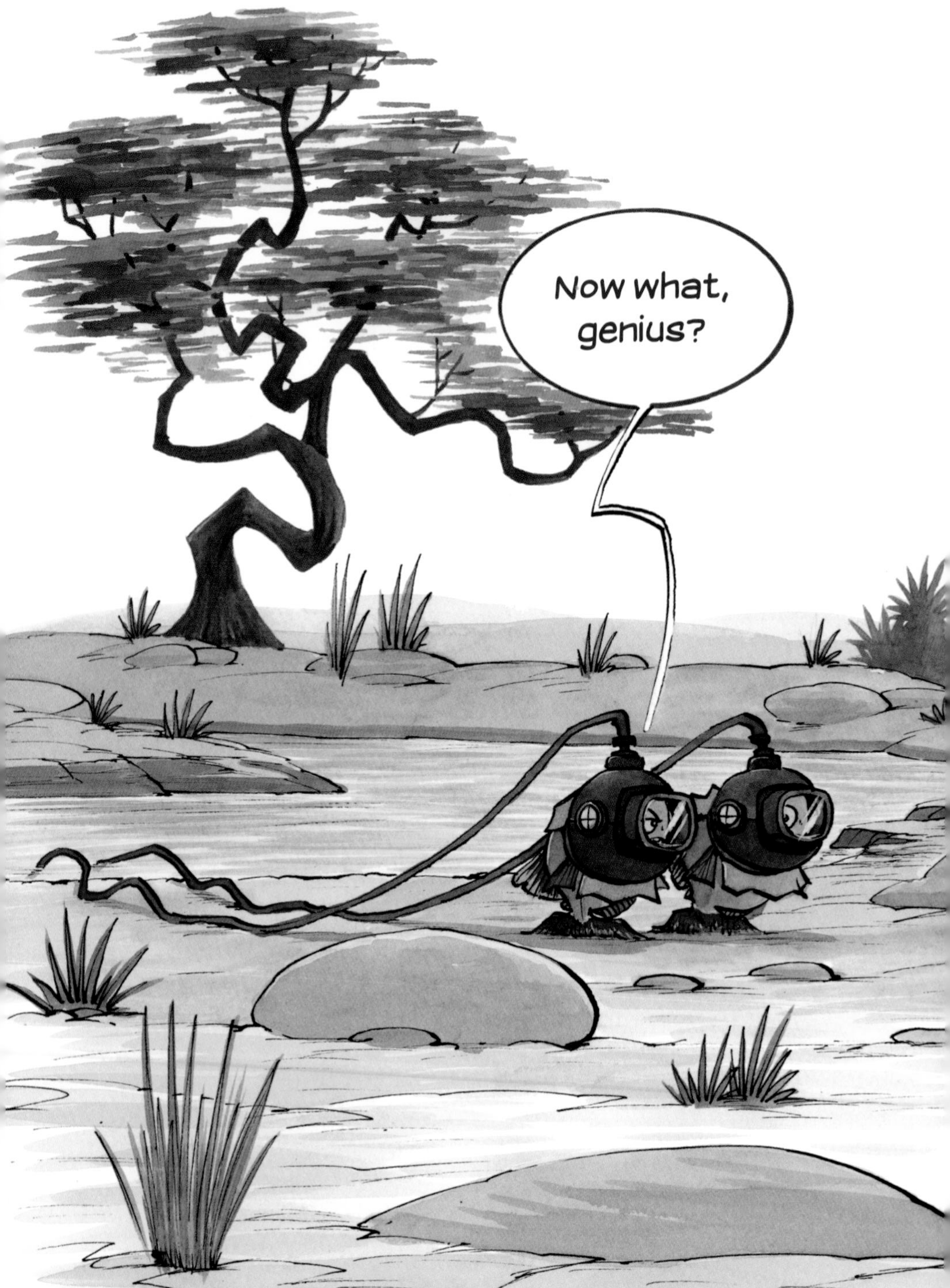
Now what, genius?

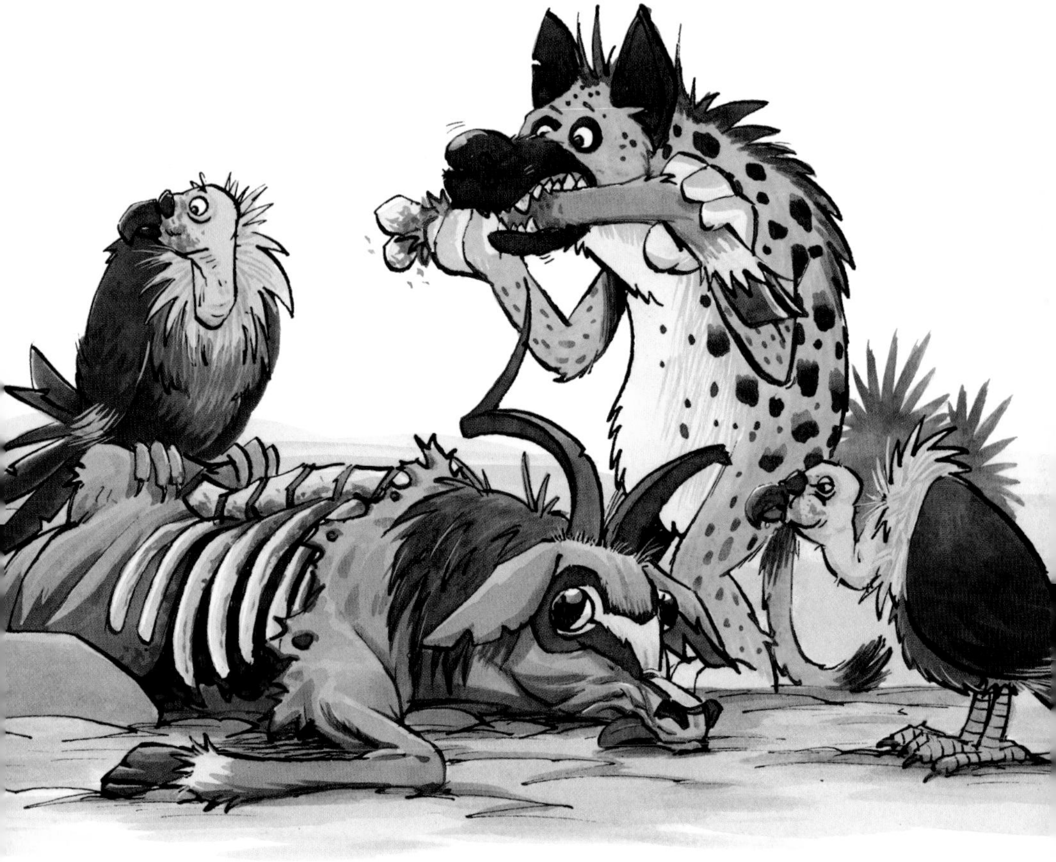

The majority of piranhas are scavengers. This means they eat dead and decaying animals.

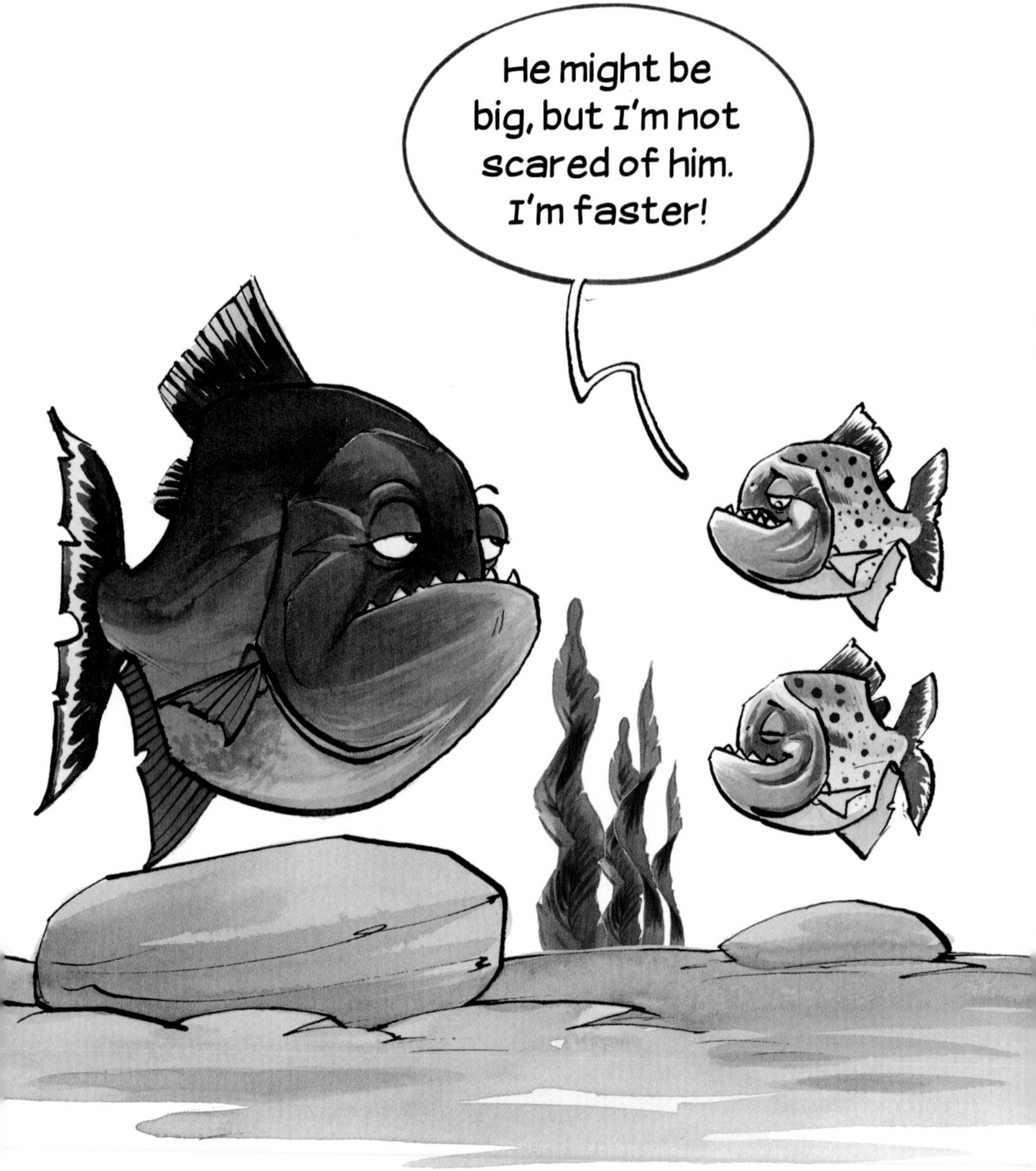
He might be big, but I'm not scared of him. I'm faster!

Many piranhas are **cannibals**.

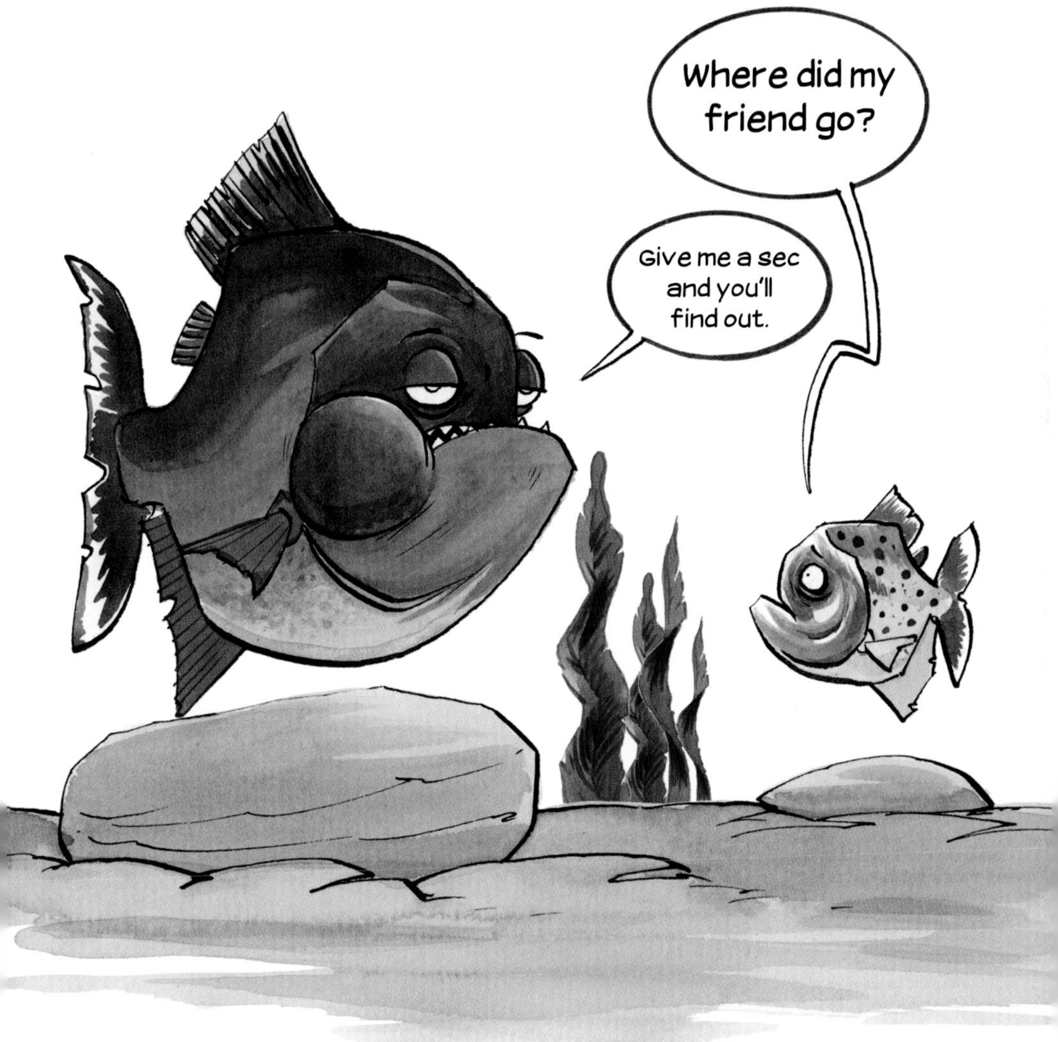
Where did my friend go?
Give me a sec and you'll find out.

For this reason, they tend to stay in groups that are similar in size in order to minimize the chances of being eaten by the bigger piranhas.

To avoid being eaten by other piranhas, they all move in the same direction and make sure that no other piranhas are directly behind them.

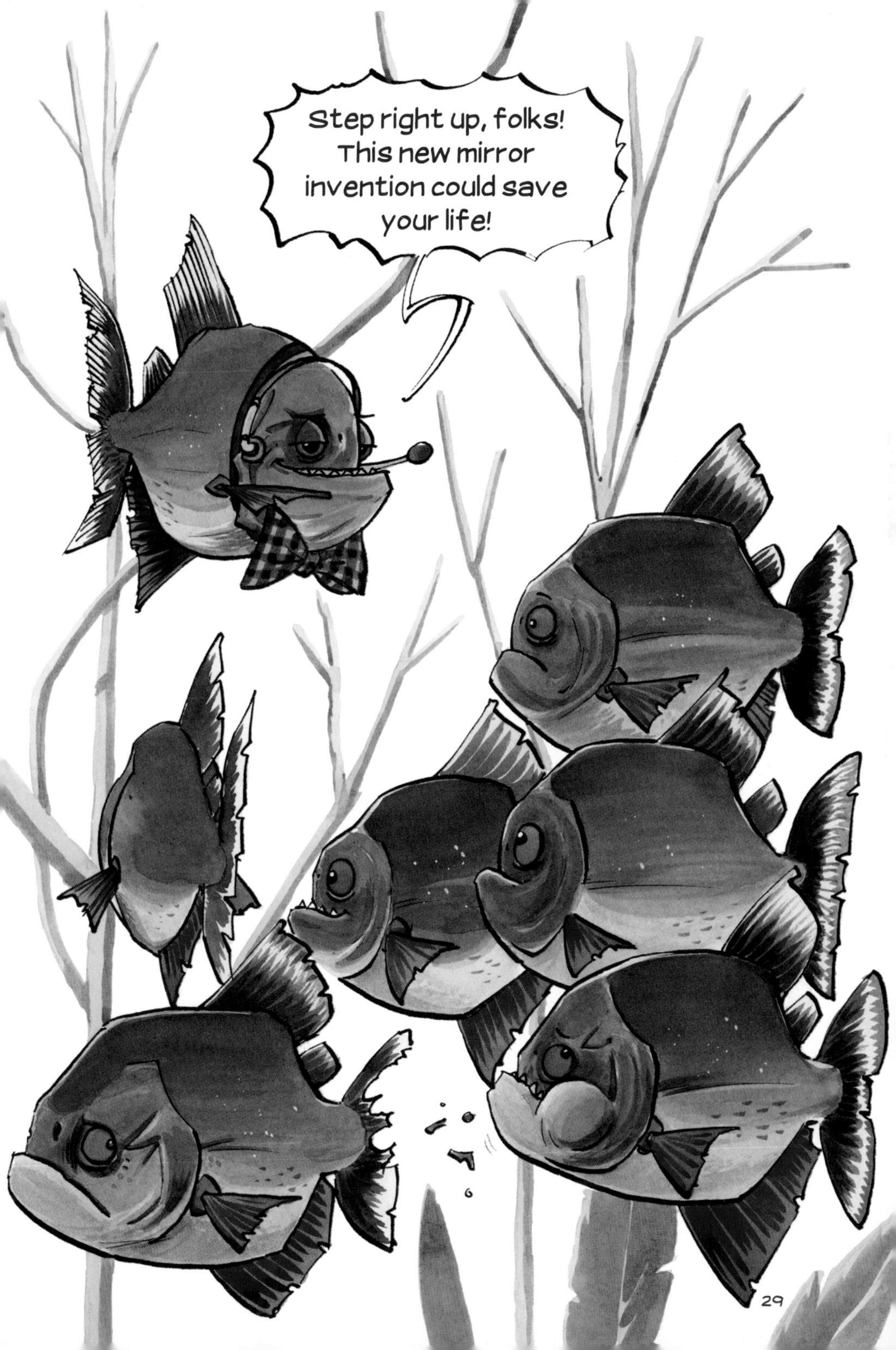
Step right up, folks! This new mirror invention could save your life!

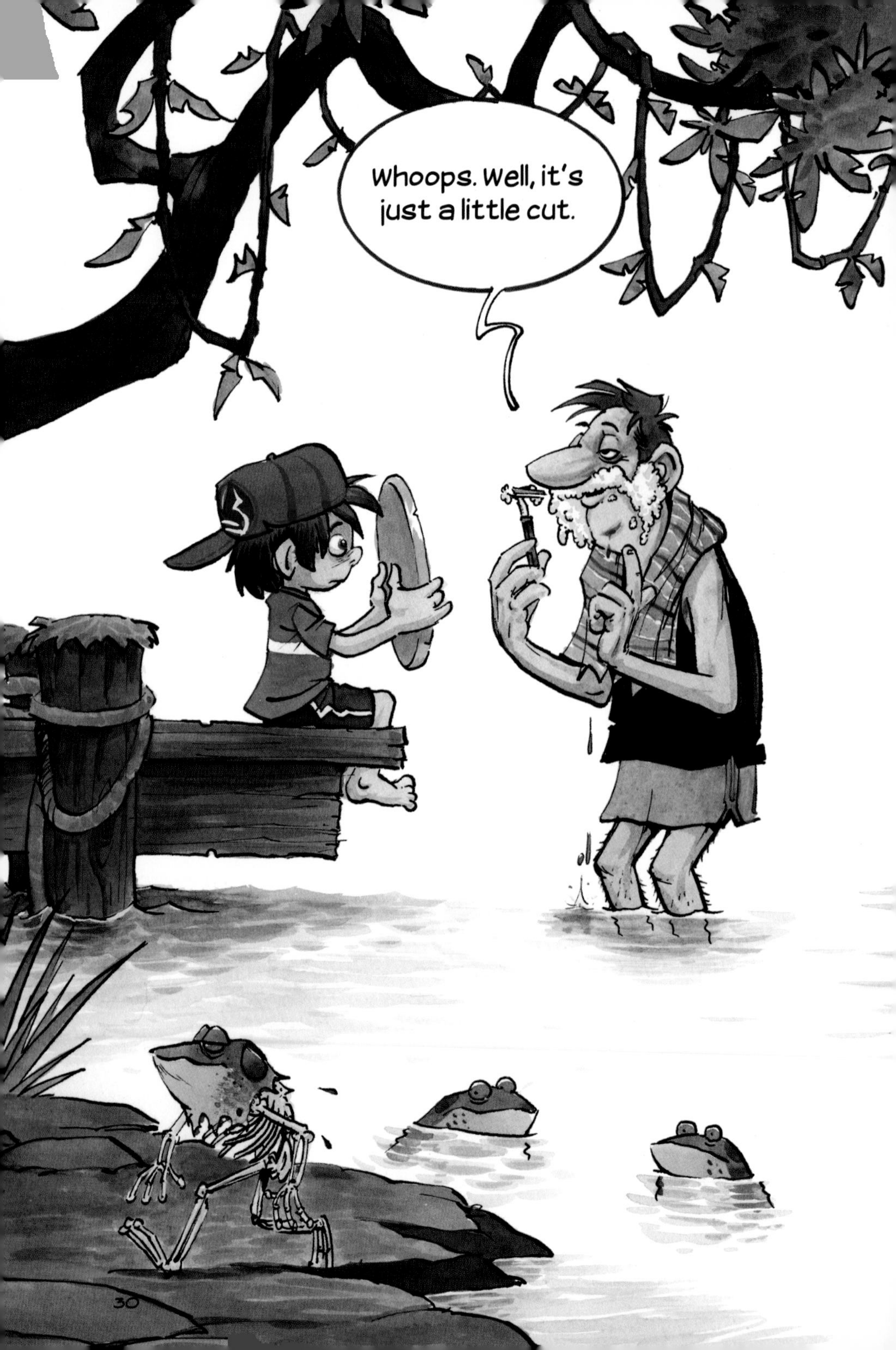
Whoops. Well, it's just a little cut.

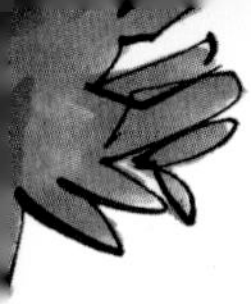

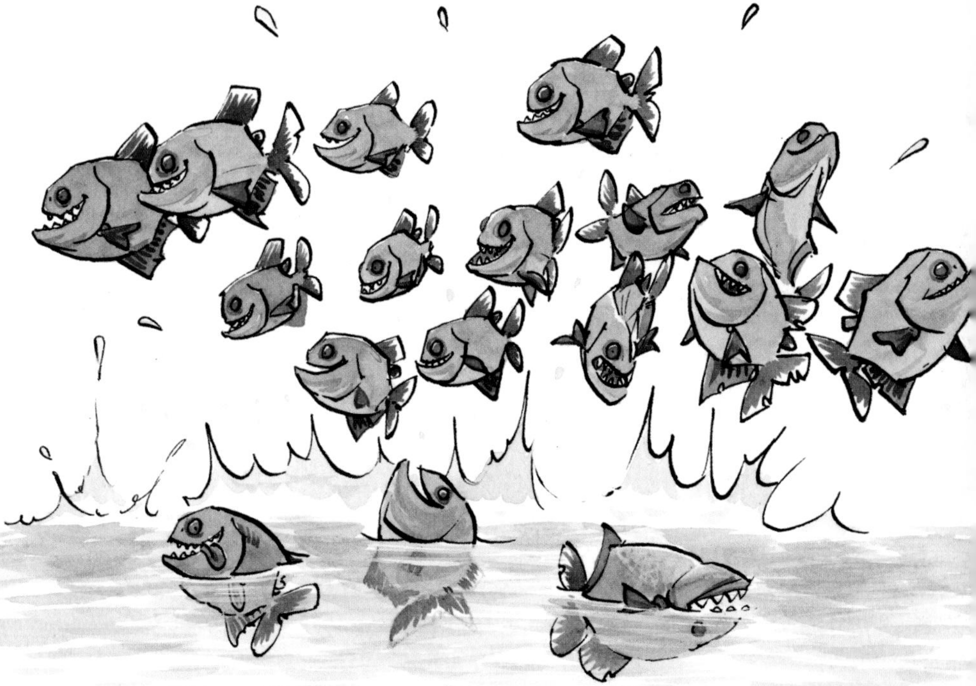

Piranhas are attracted to the scent of blood. This odour makes them frantic.

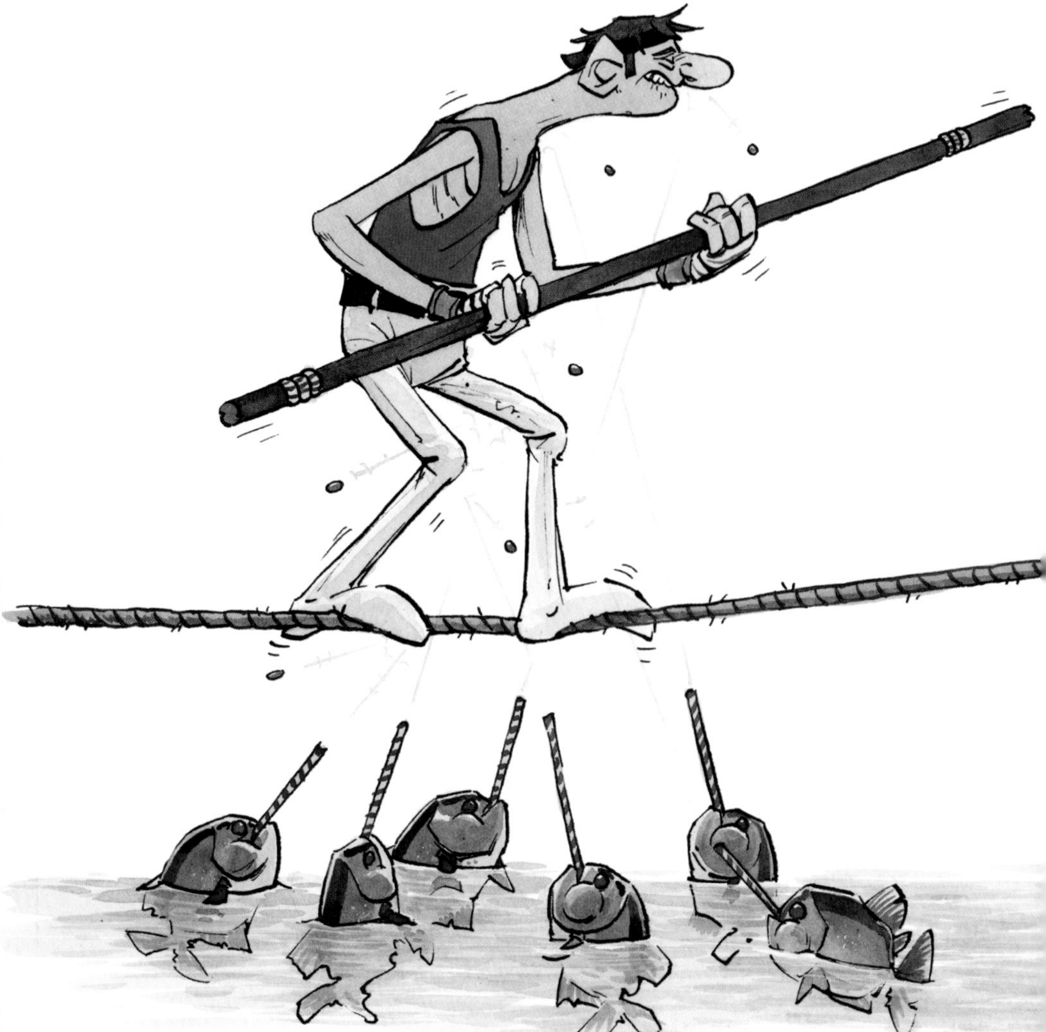

Piranhas are also attracted to quick movements in the water. They can immediately detect anything that falls in the water.

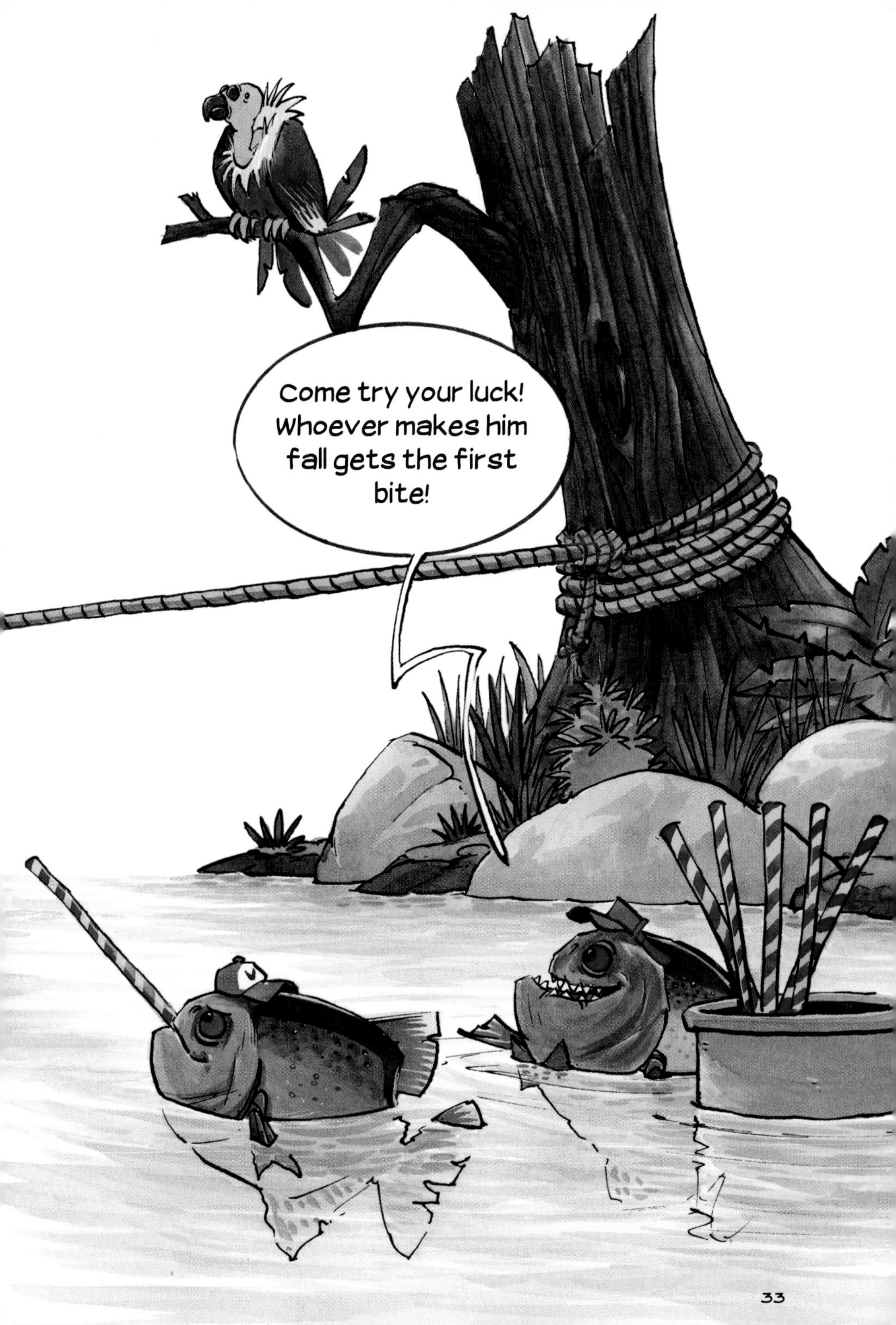
Come try your luck! Whoever makes him fall gets the first bite!

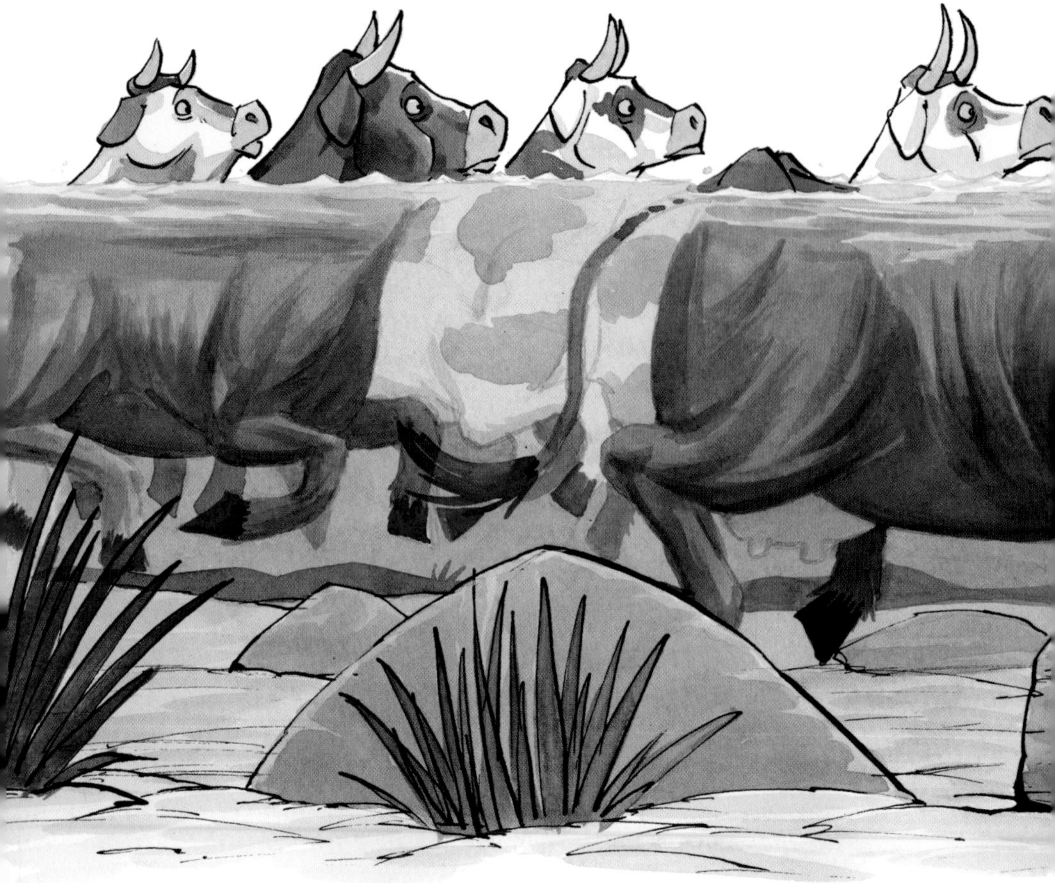

In just a few minutes, piranhas can devour a cow that has fallen in the water, leaving nothing but a skeleton behind.

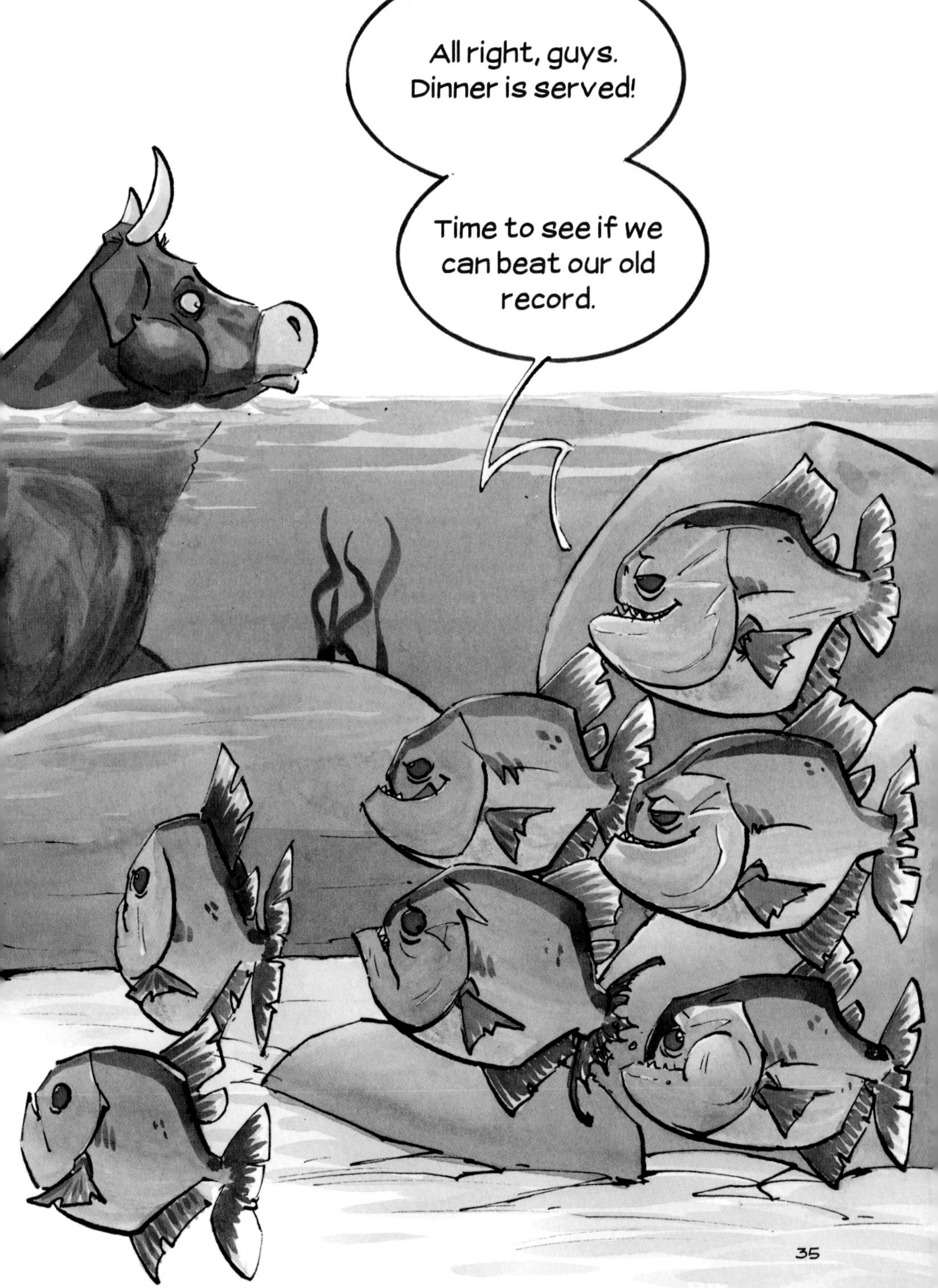
All right, guys. Dinner is served!
Time to see if we can beat our old record.

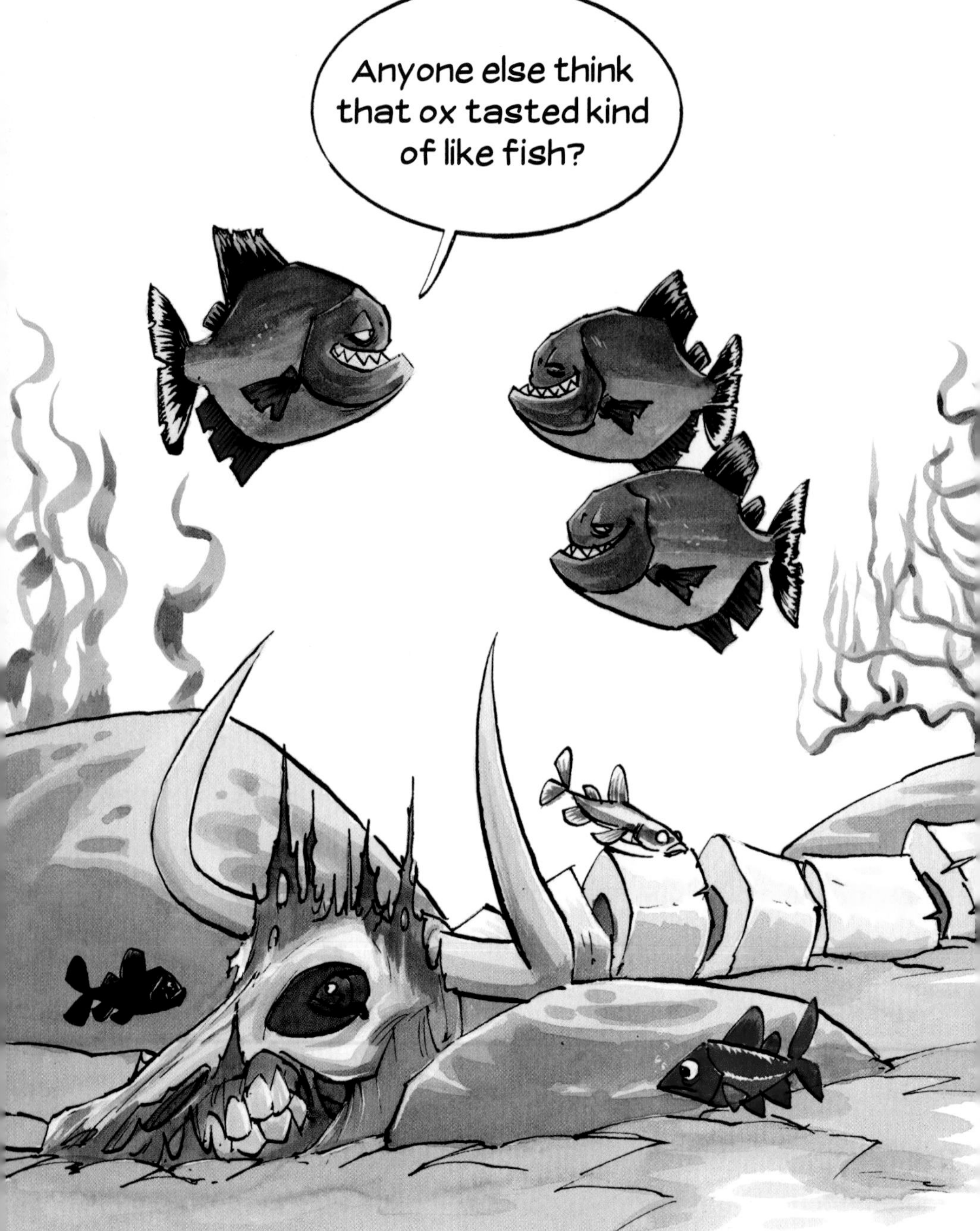
Anyone else think that ox tasted kind of like fish?

While eating, piranhas often bite each other.

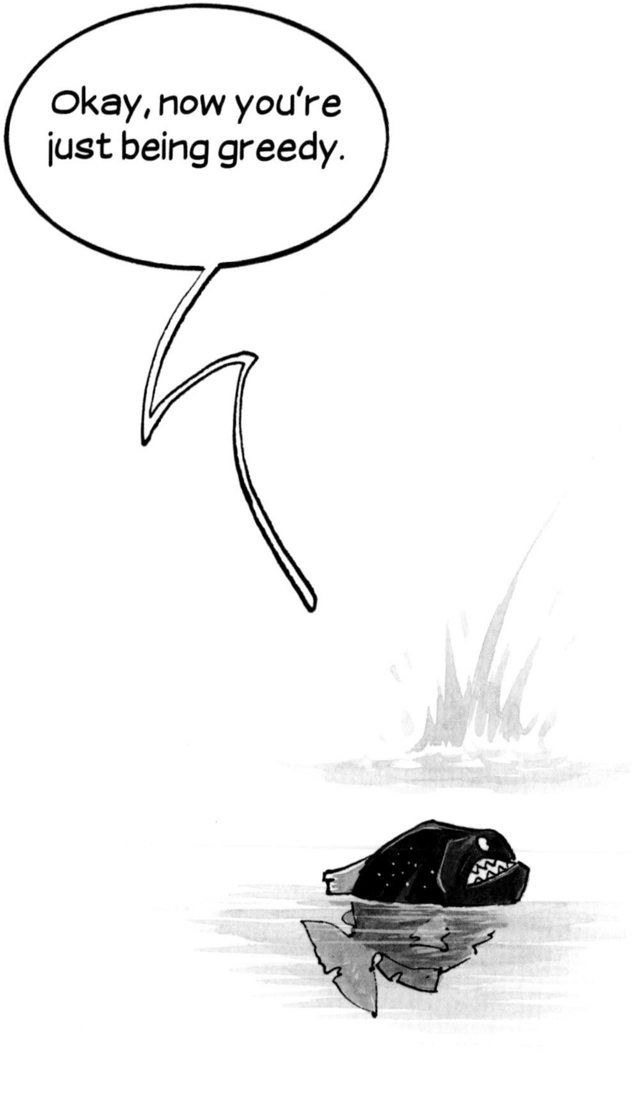
Okay, now you're just being greedy.

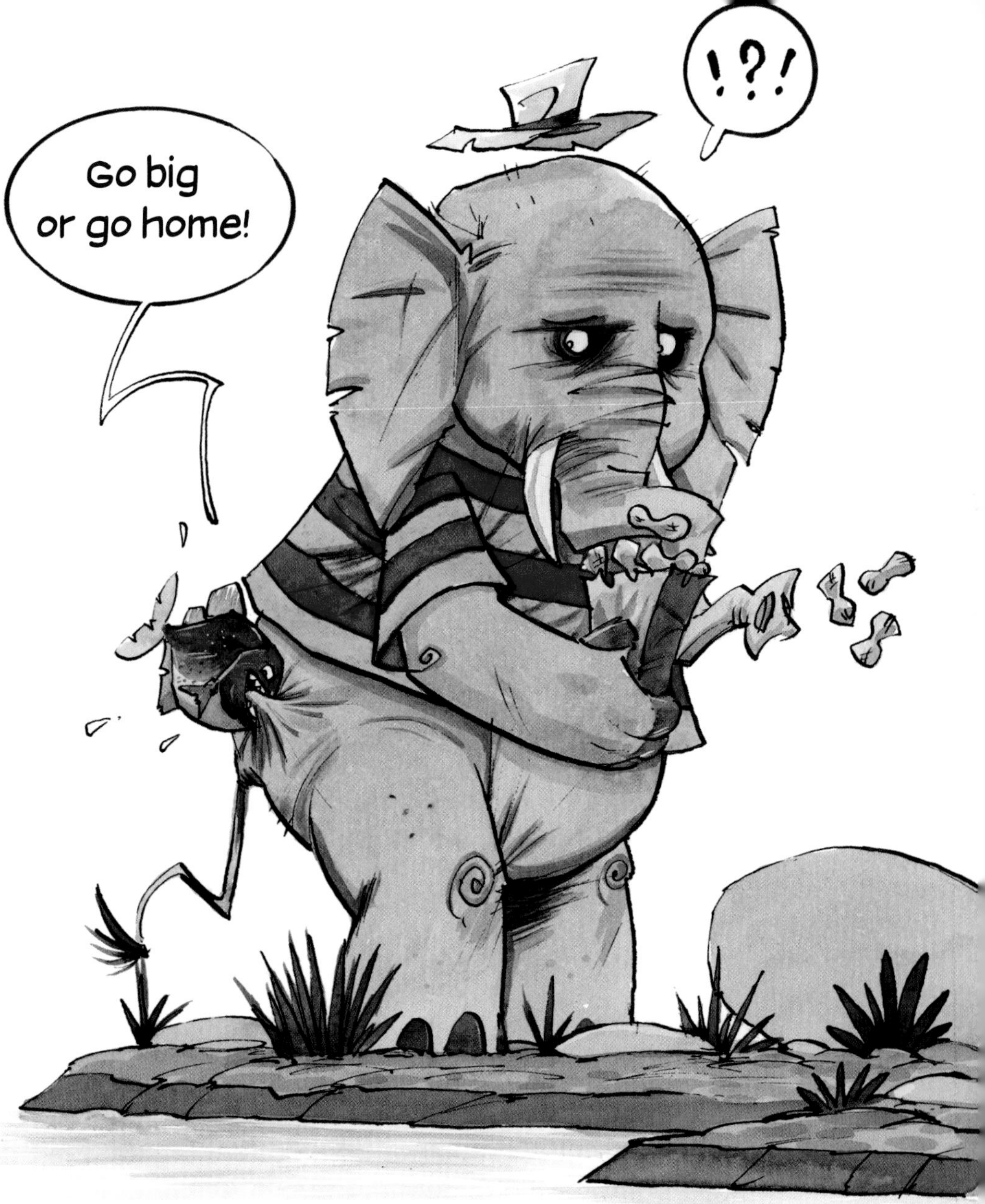
Go big or go home!
!?!

Often, a piranha will jump out of the water to catch its **prey**.

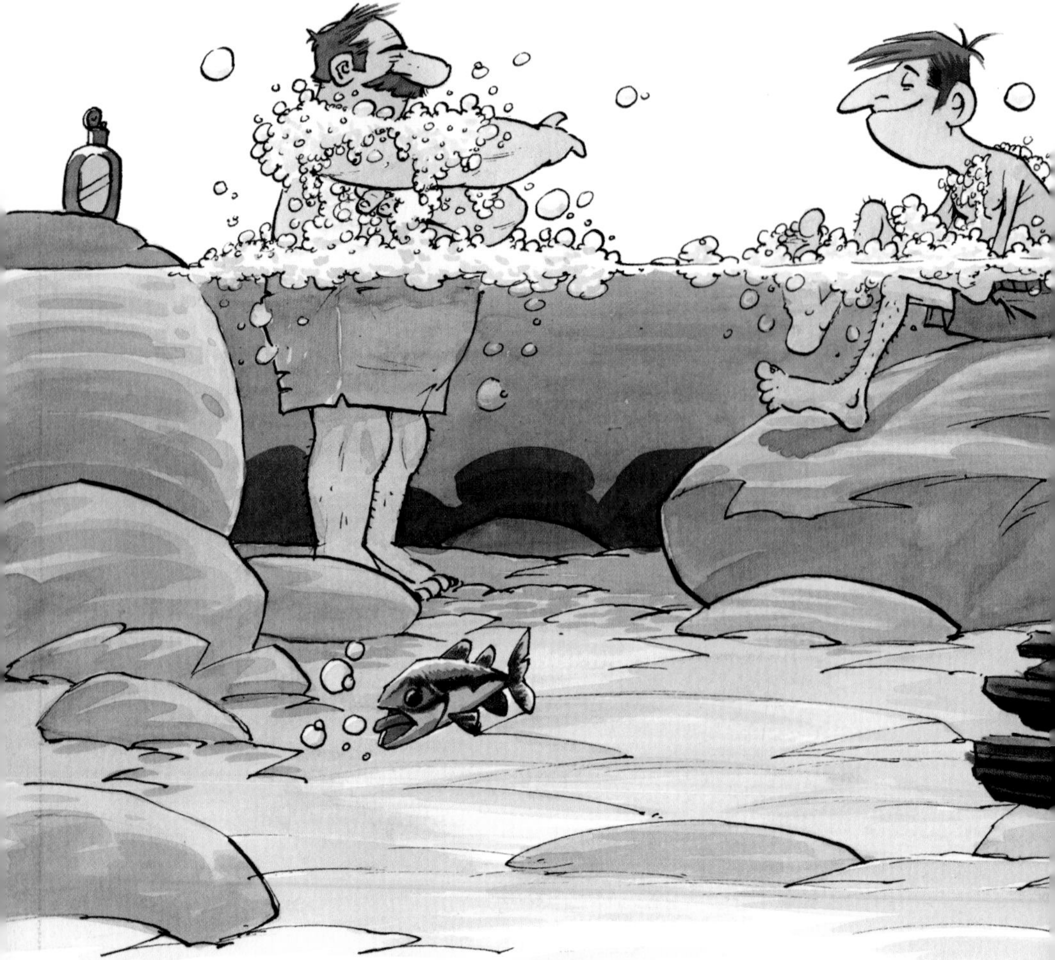

Only a few species can attack large animals, such as humans.

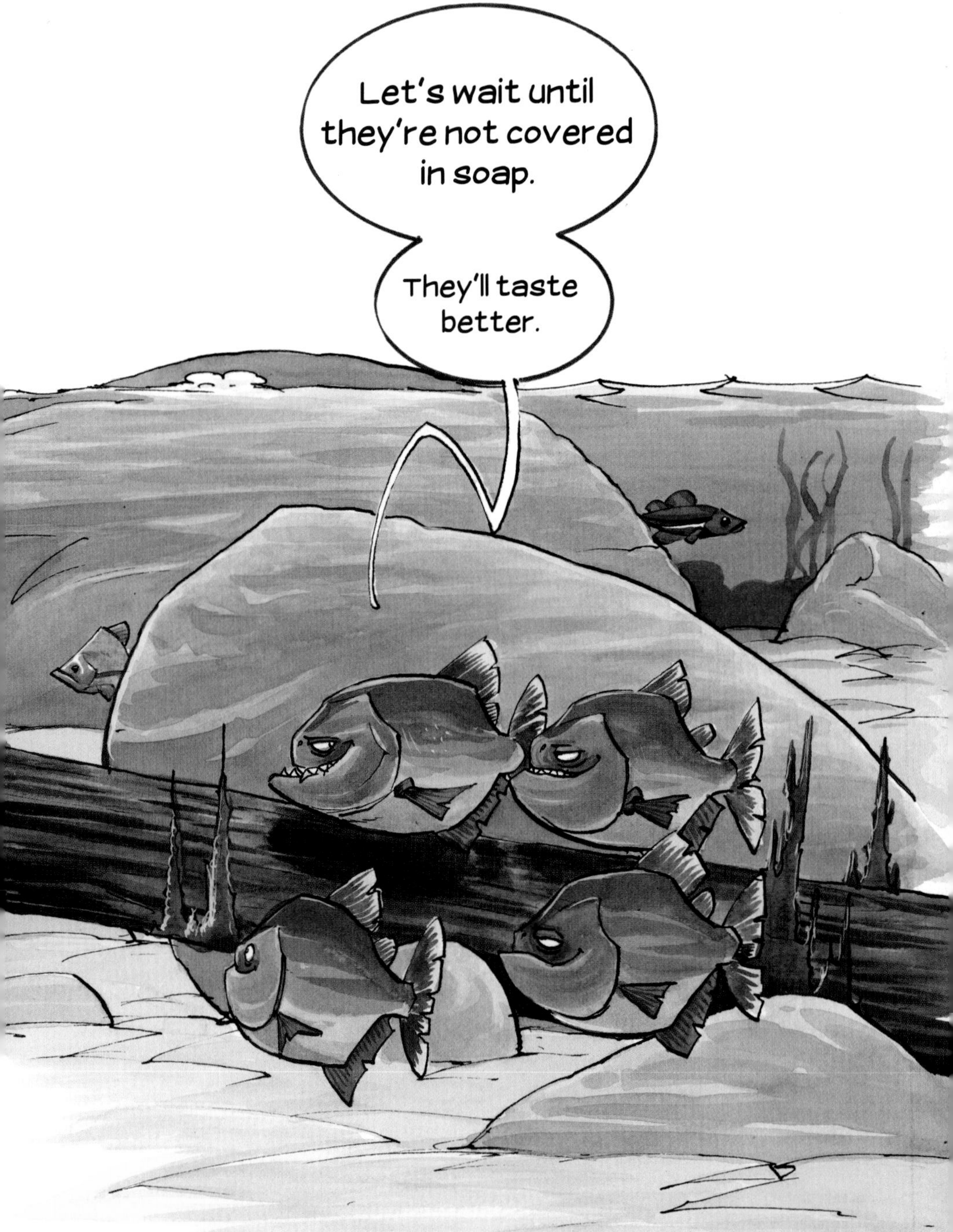
Let's wait until they're not covered in soap.
They'll taste better.

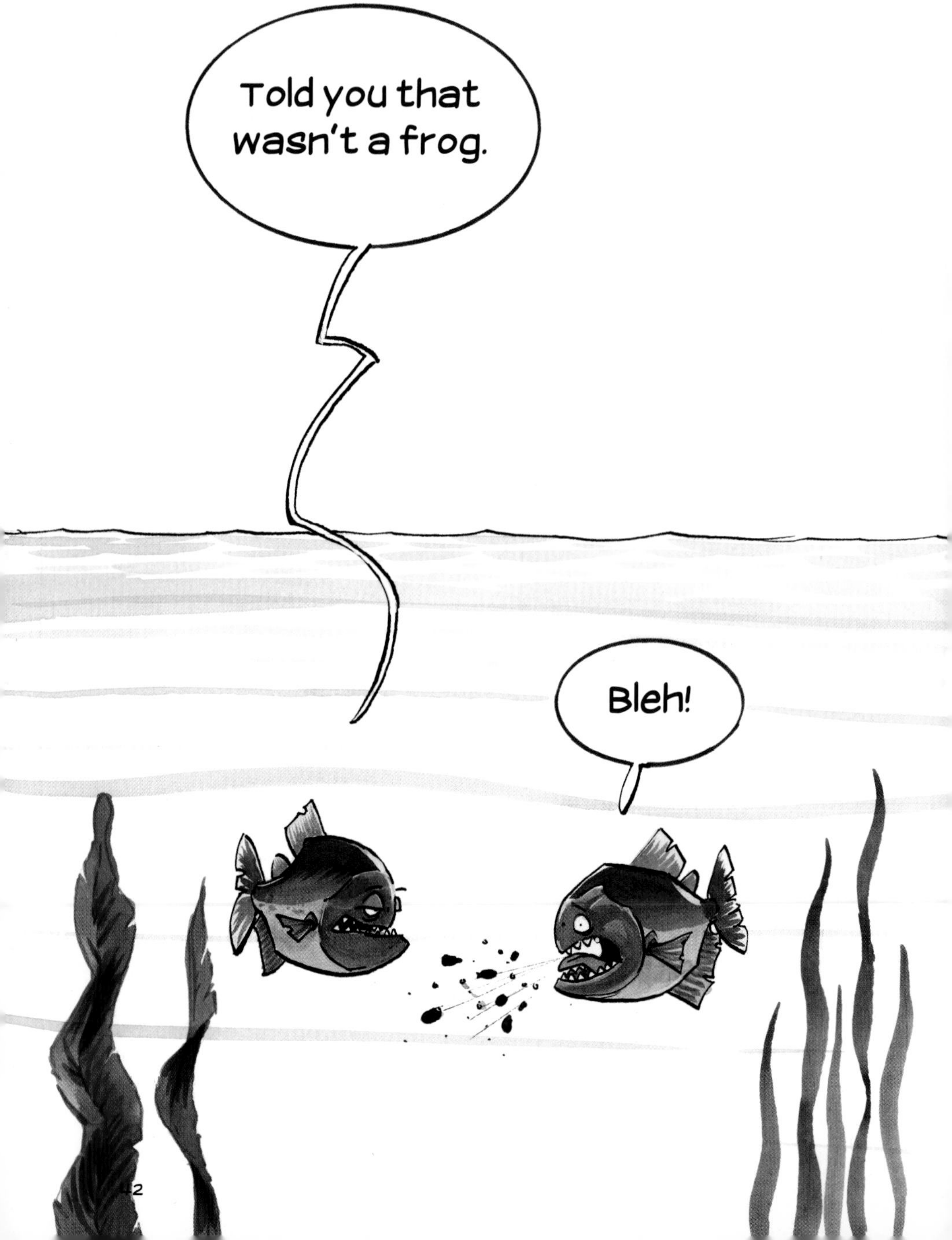
Told you that wasn't a frog.
Bleh!

Piranhas' aggression towards humans has been exaggerated. No serious proof exists of a human being killed by piranhas.

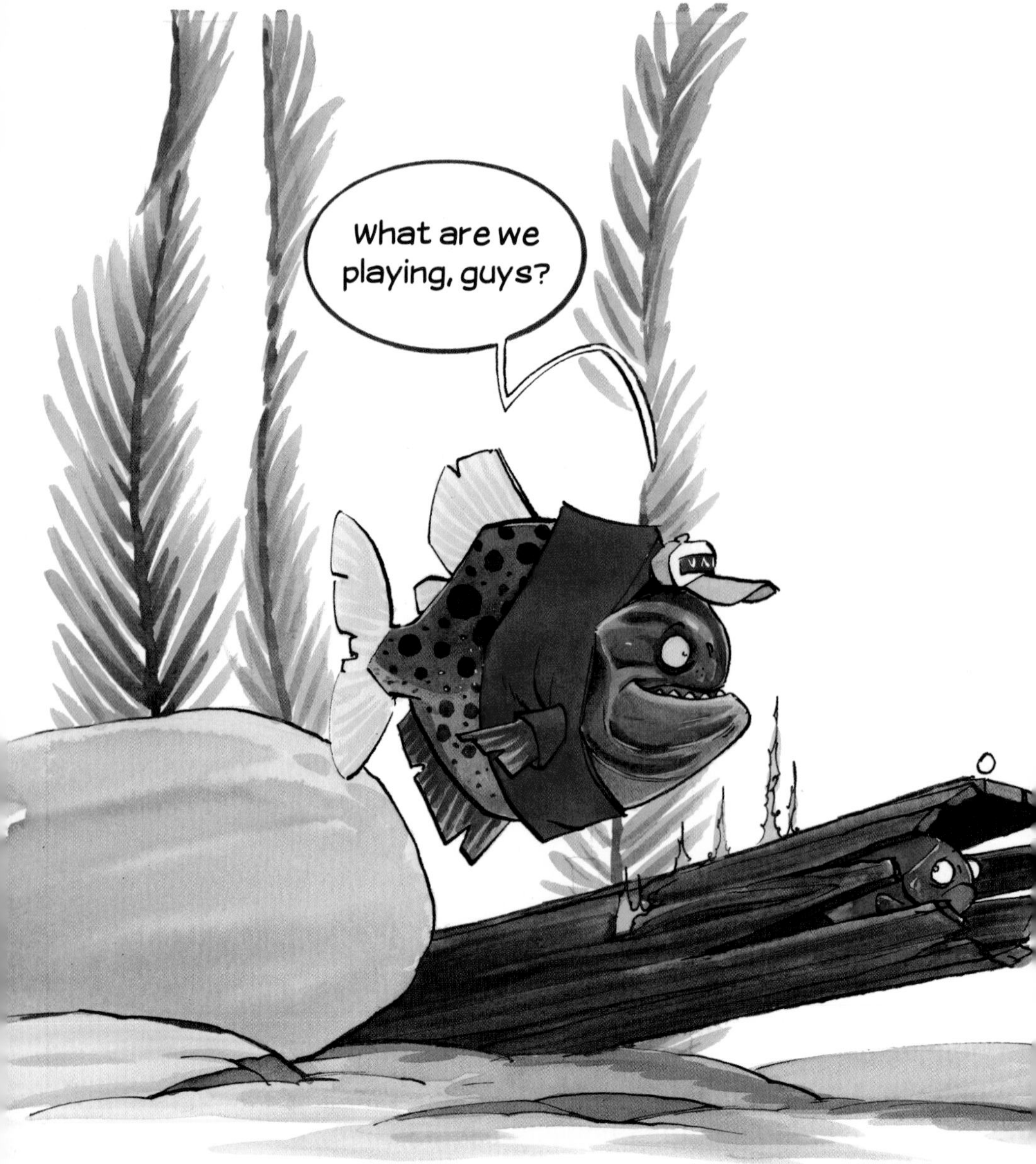
What are we playing, guys?

Although some species can be dangerous, most are harmless.

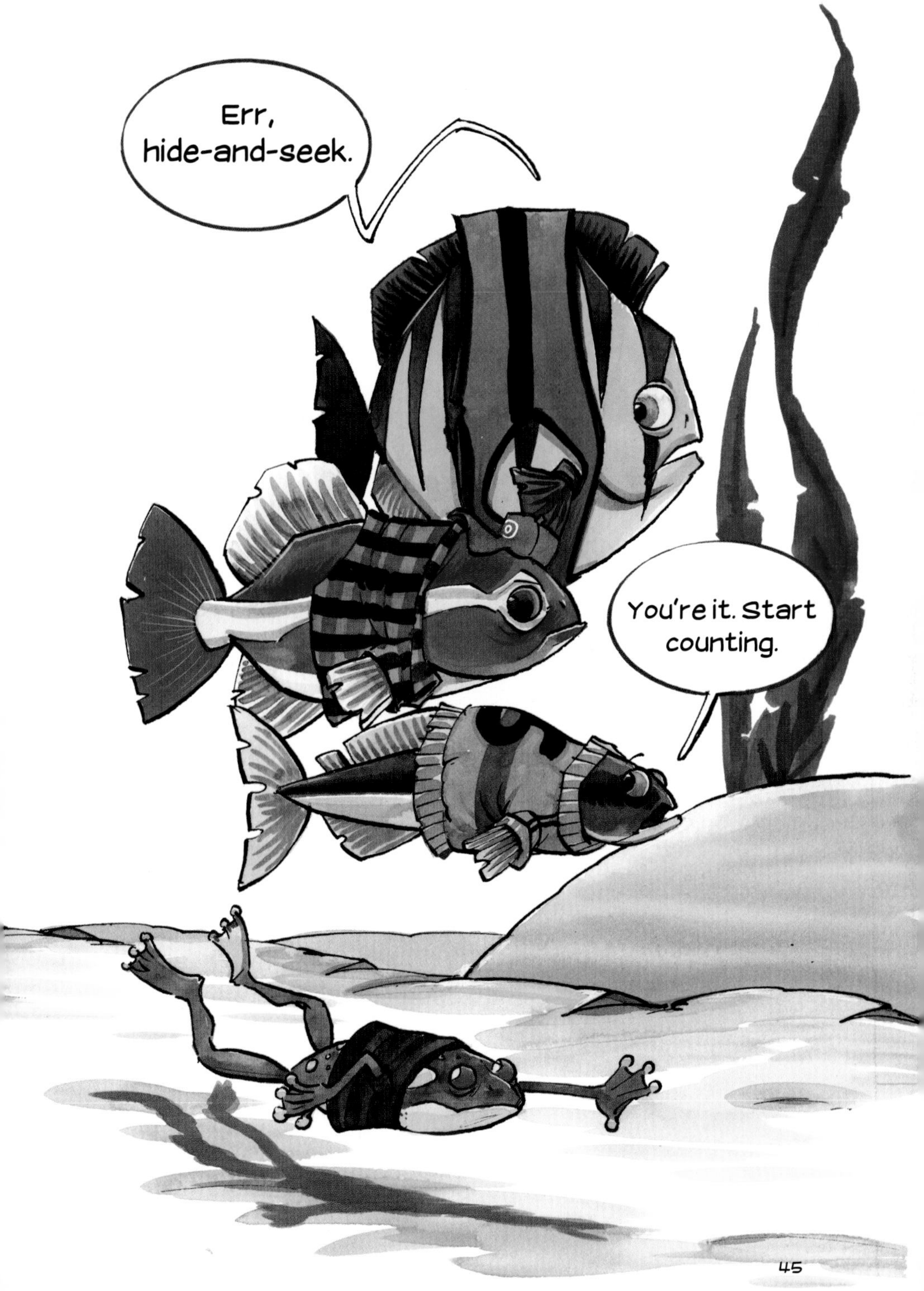
Err, hide-and-seek.
You're it. Start counting.

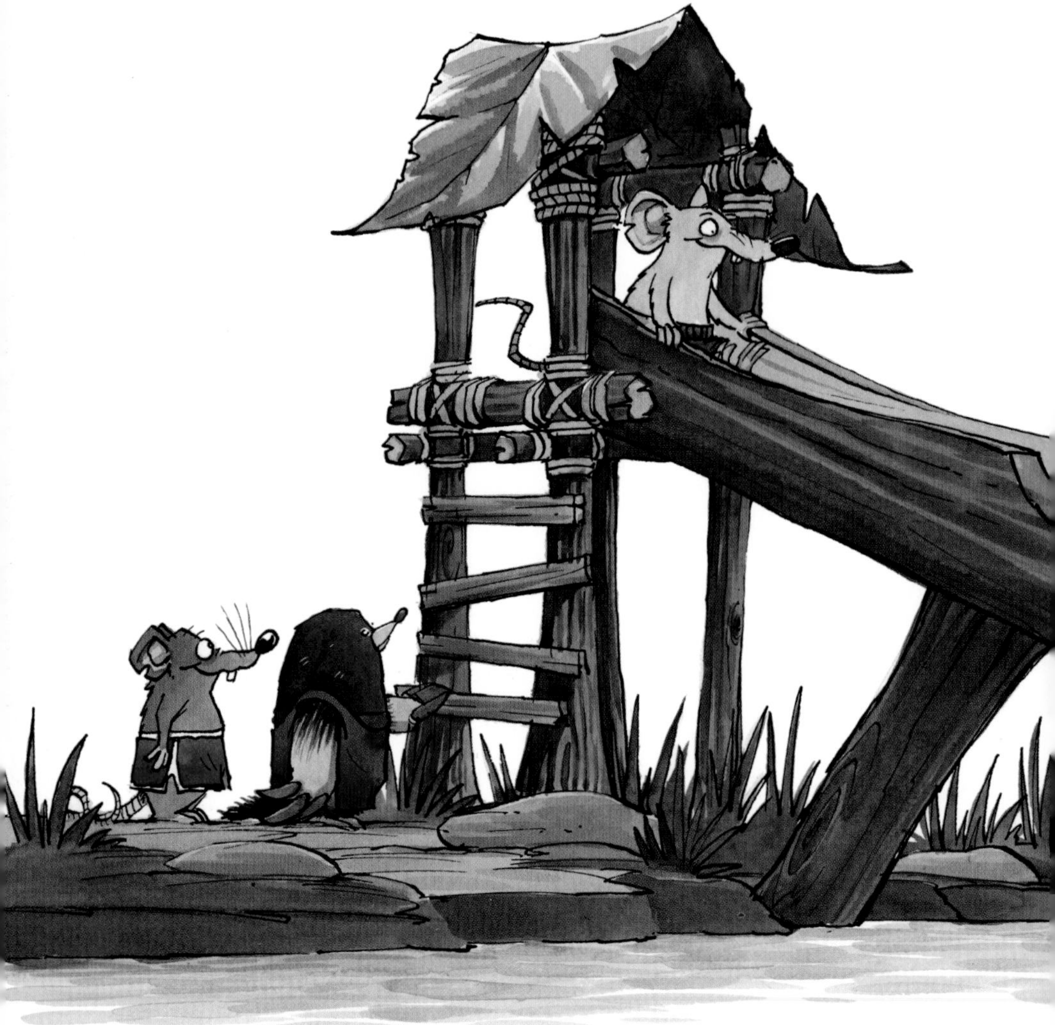

Each species has a different way of hunting. Some prefer to **ambush** their prey, some fake disinterest before attacking, while others prefer the chase.

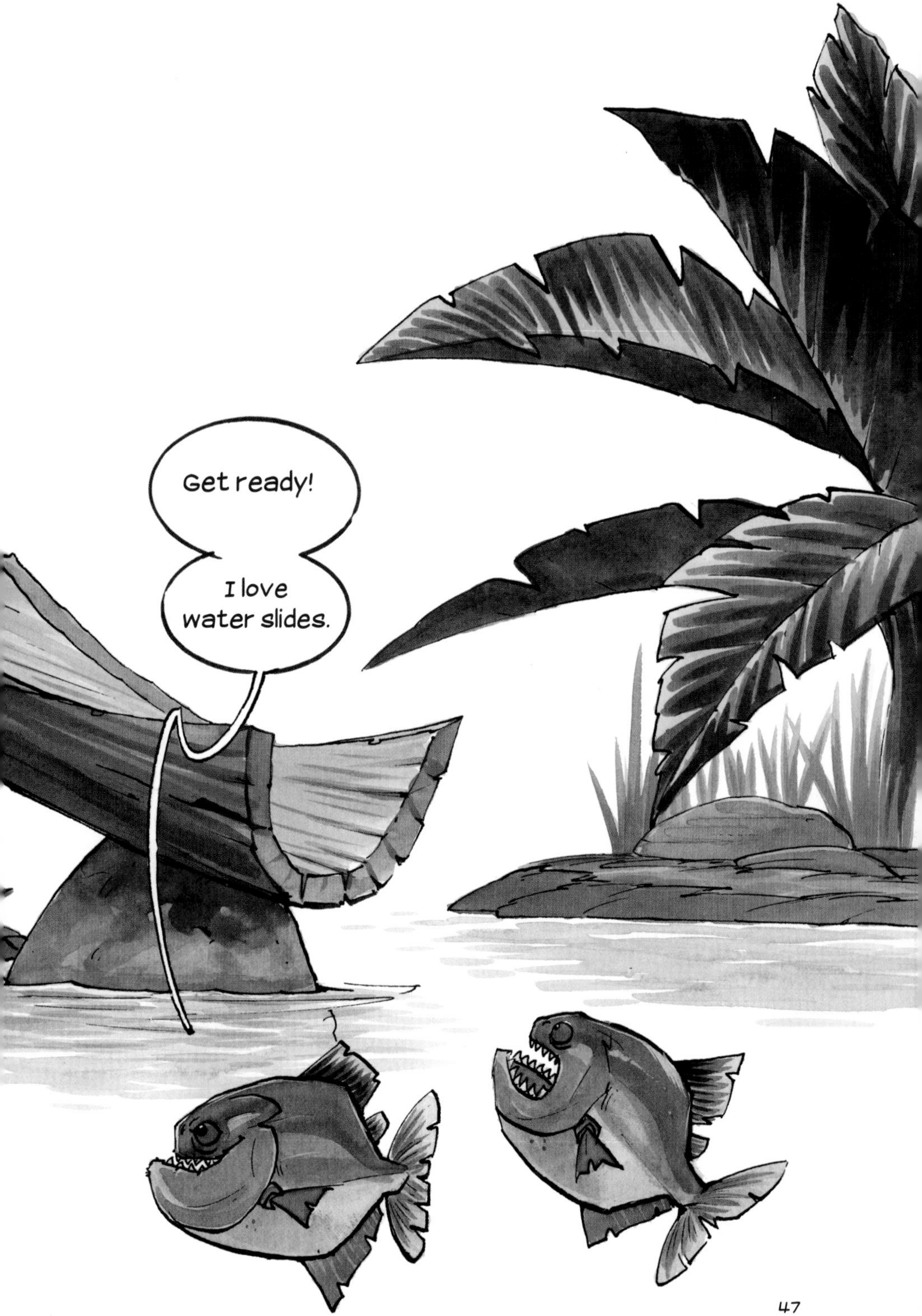
Get ready!
I love water slides.

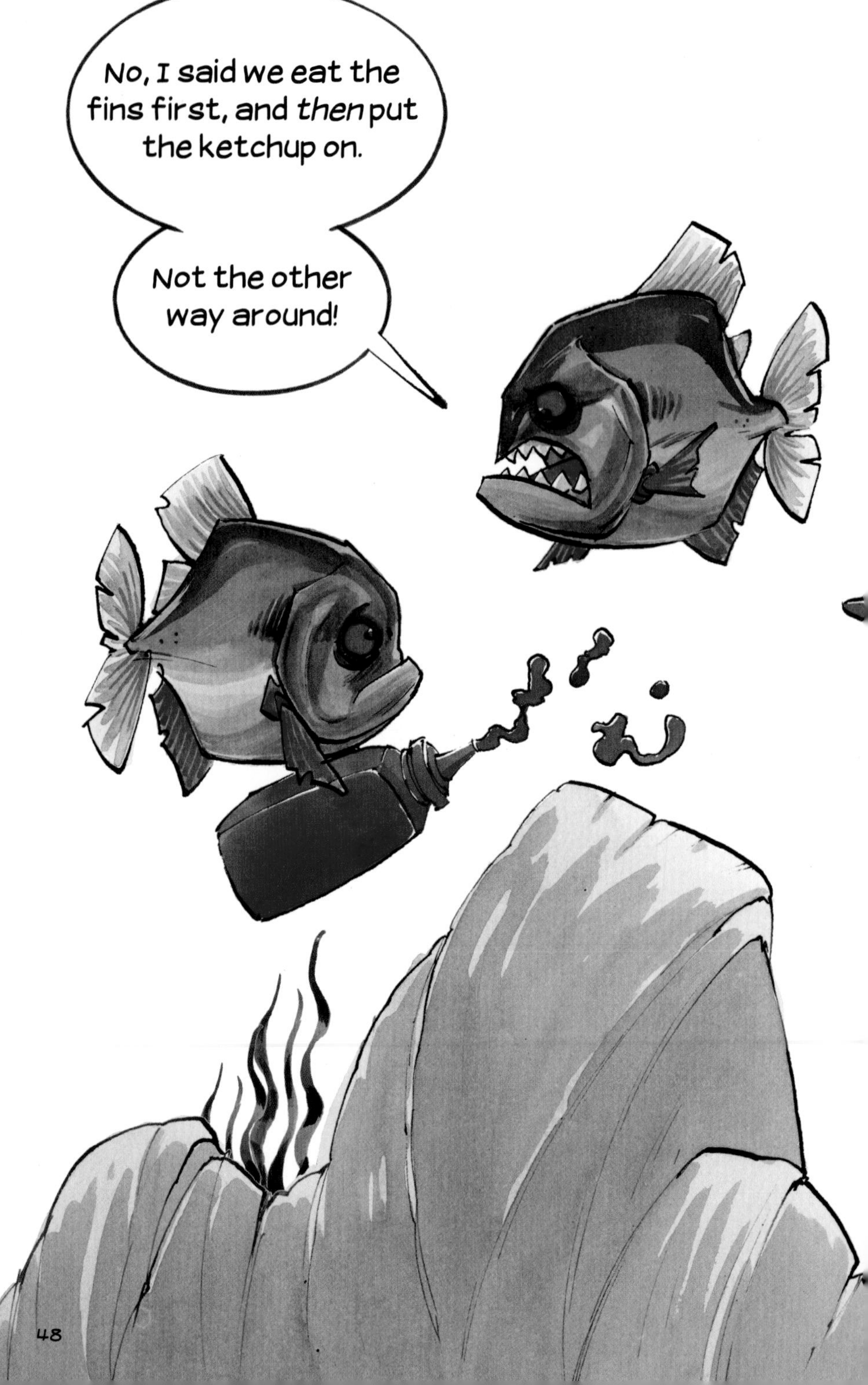
No, I said we eat the fins first, and *then* put the ketchup on.
Not the other way around!

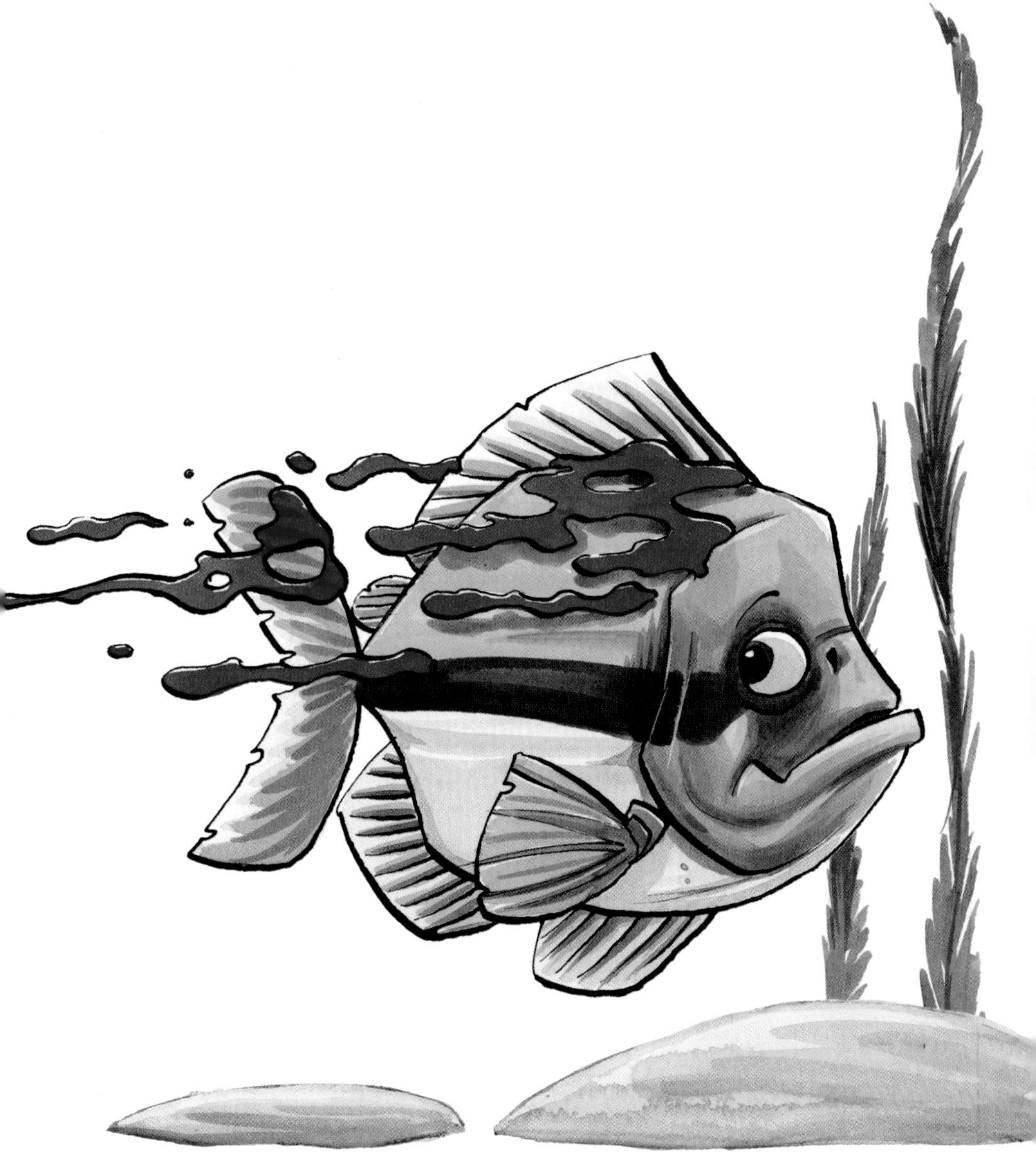

To catch their prey, piranhas will first eat the tail fins. Some scientists believe piranhas use this hunting tactic to stop the prey from being able to escape.

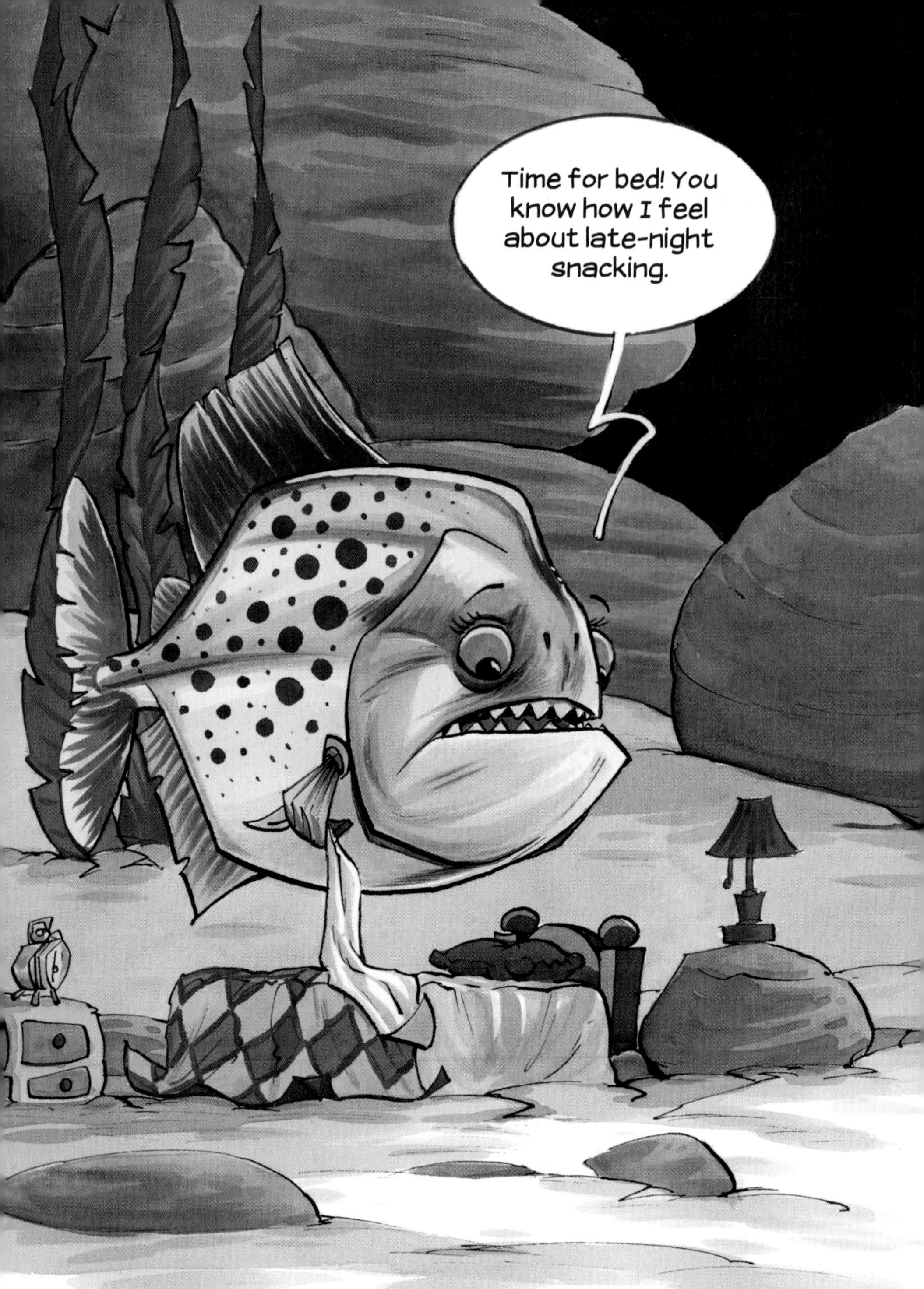
Time for bed! You know how I feel about late-night snacking.

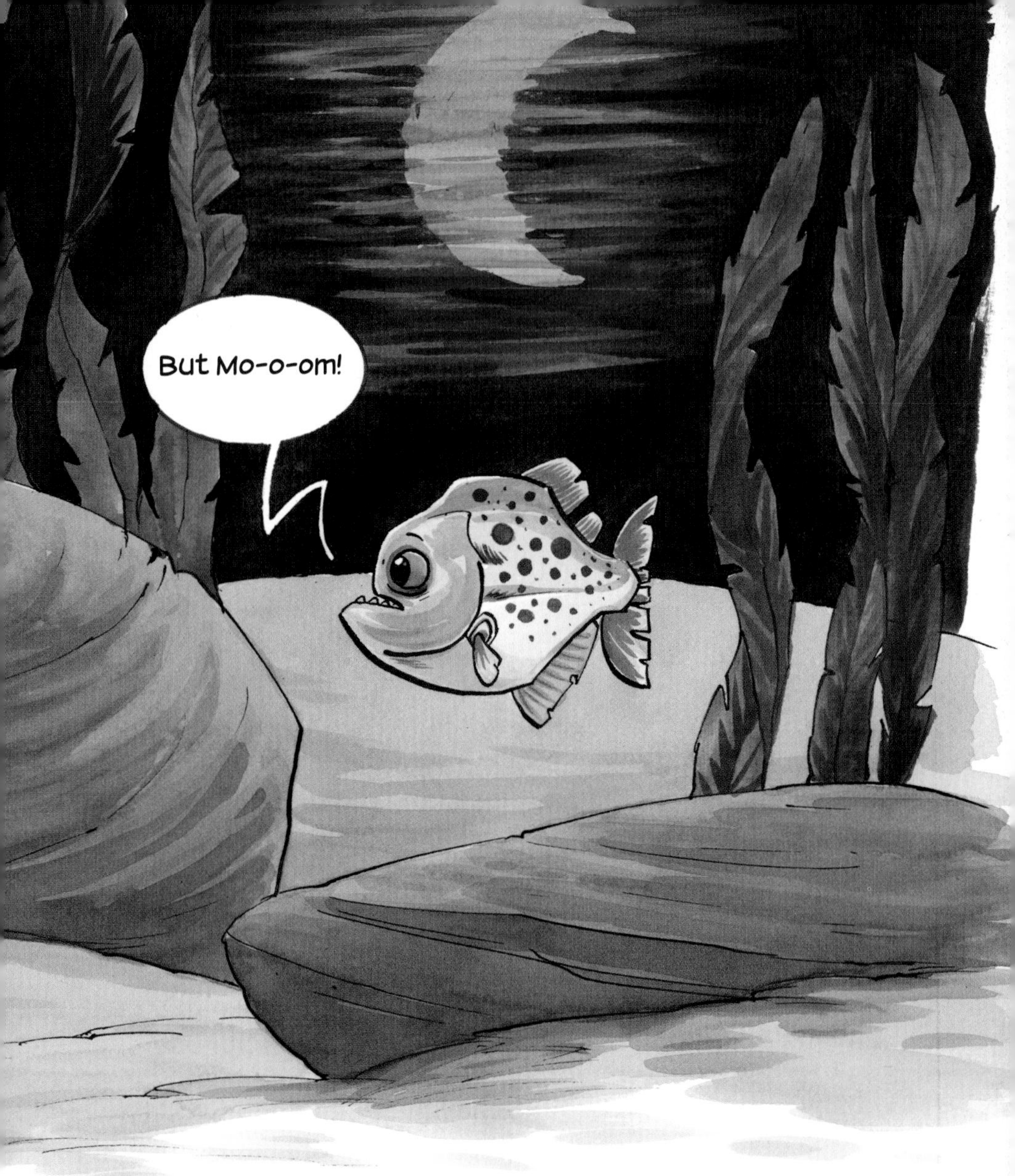
But Mo-o-om!

Piranhas are only active during the day. At night, they rest while hiding in vegetation.

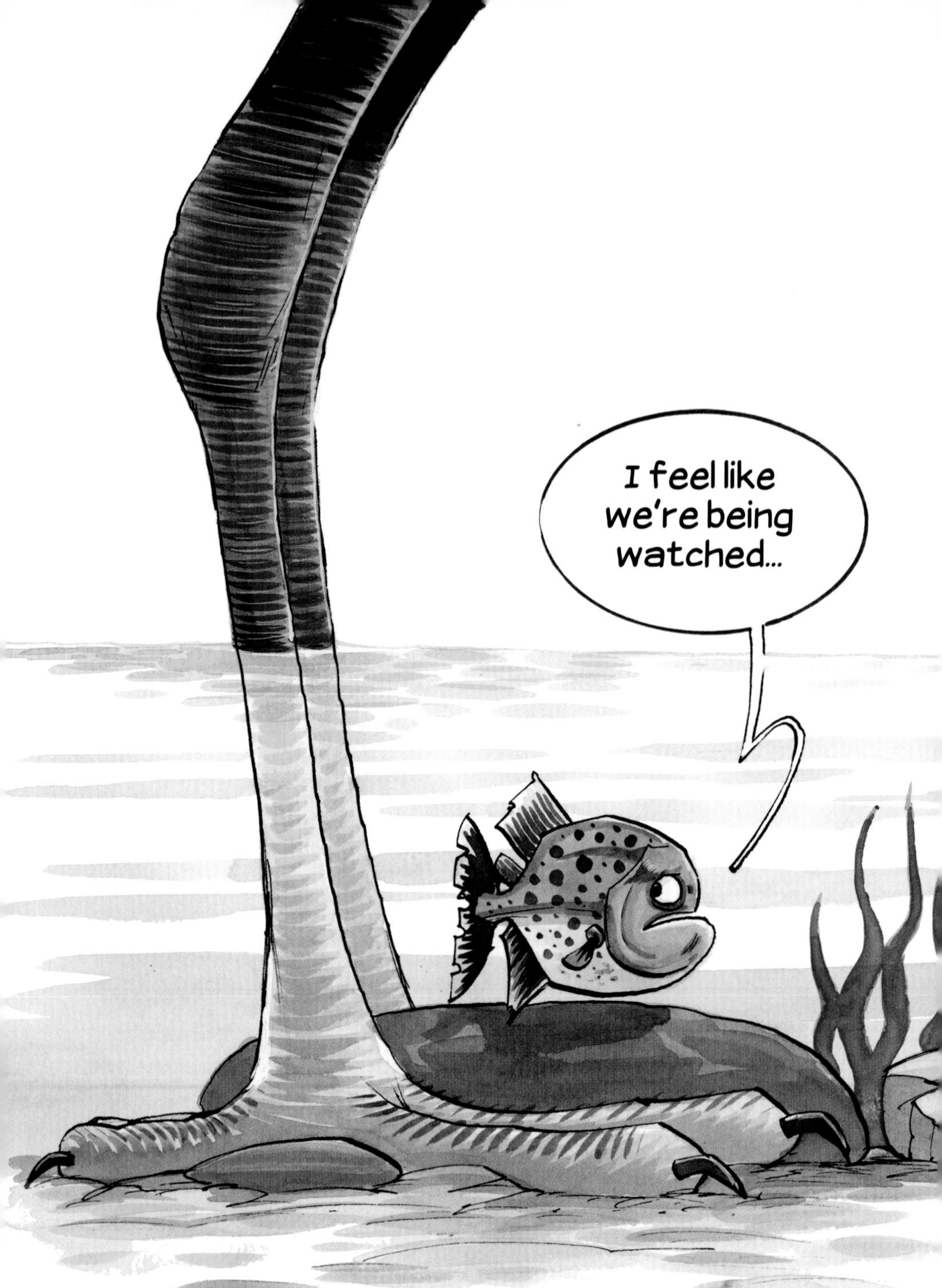
I feel like we're being watched...

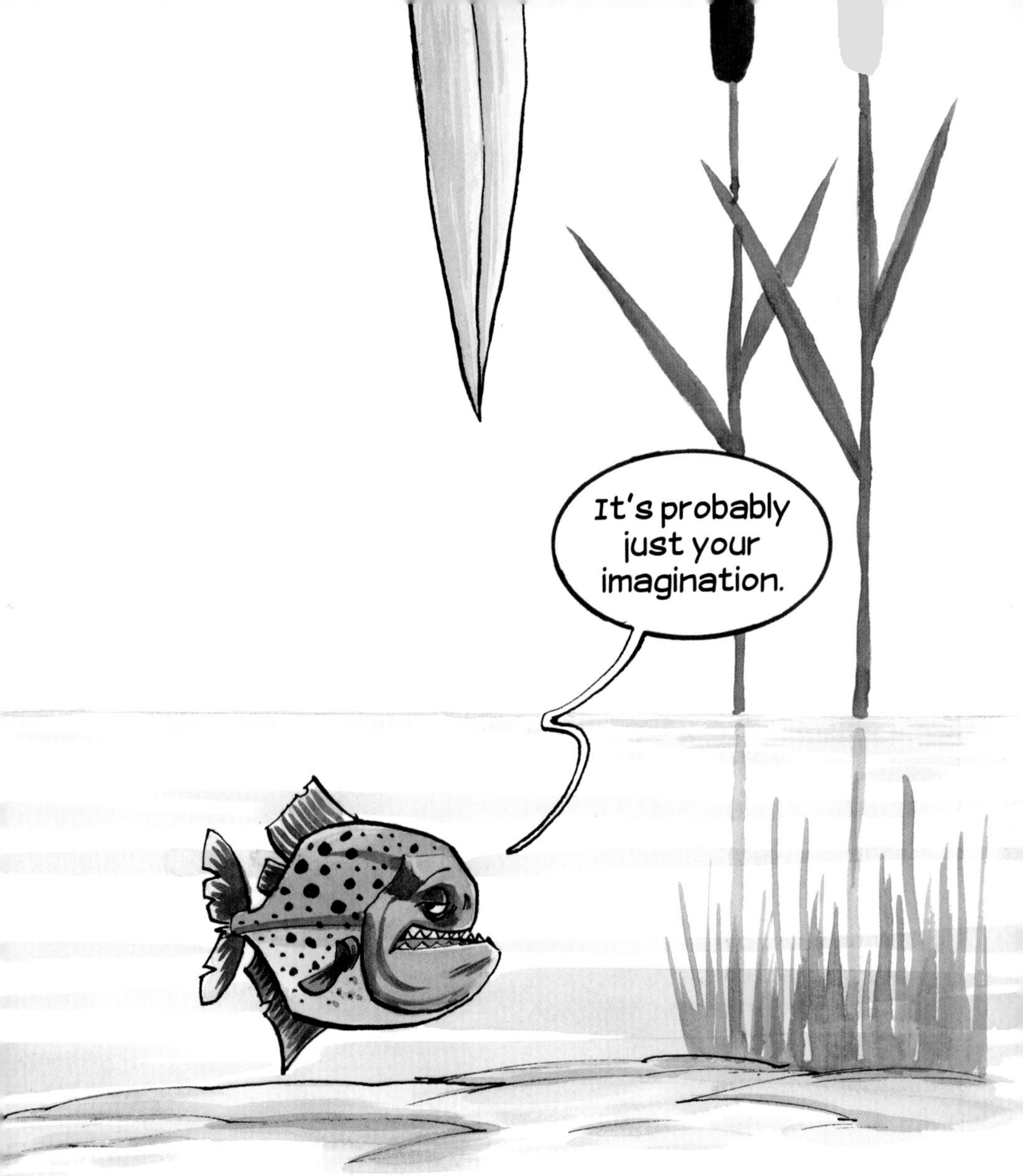
It's probably just your imagination.

Smaller species of piranhas often become the prey of many different species of birds and fish.

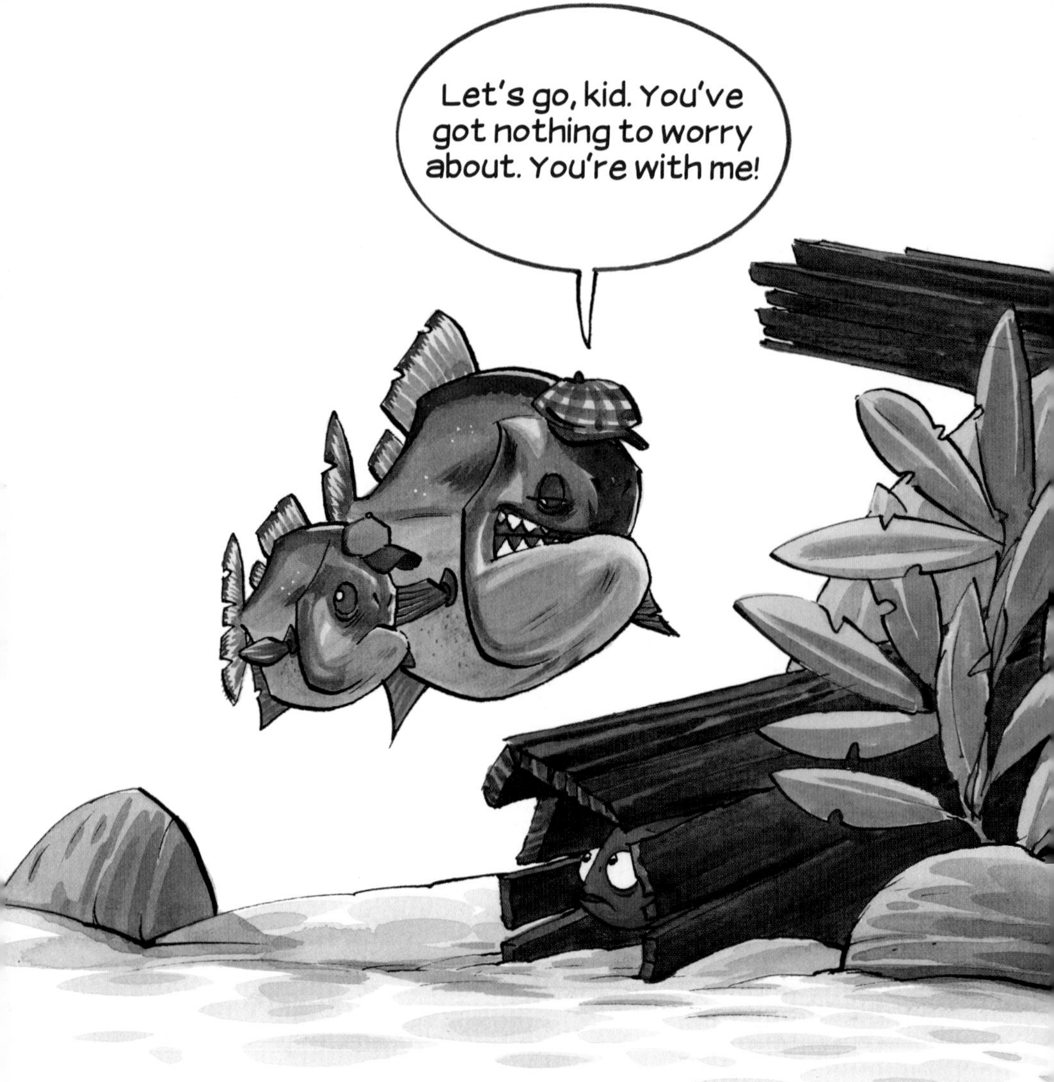
Let's go, kid. You've got nothing to worry about. You're with me!

Apart from **caimans**, humans, and other piranhas, the larger species have very few enemies.

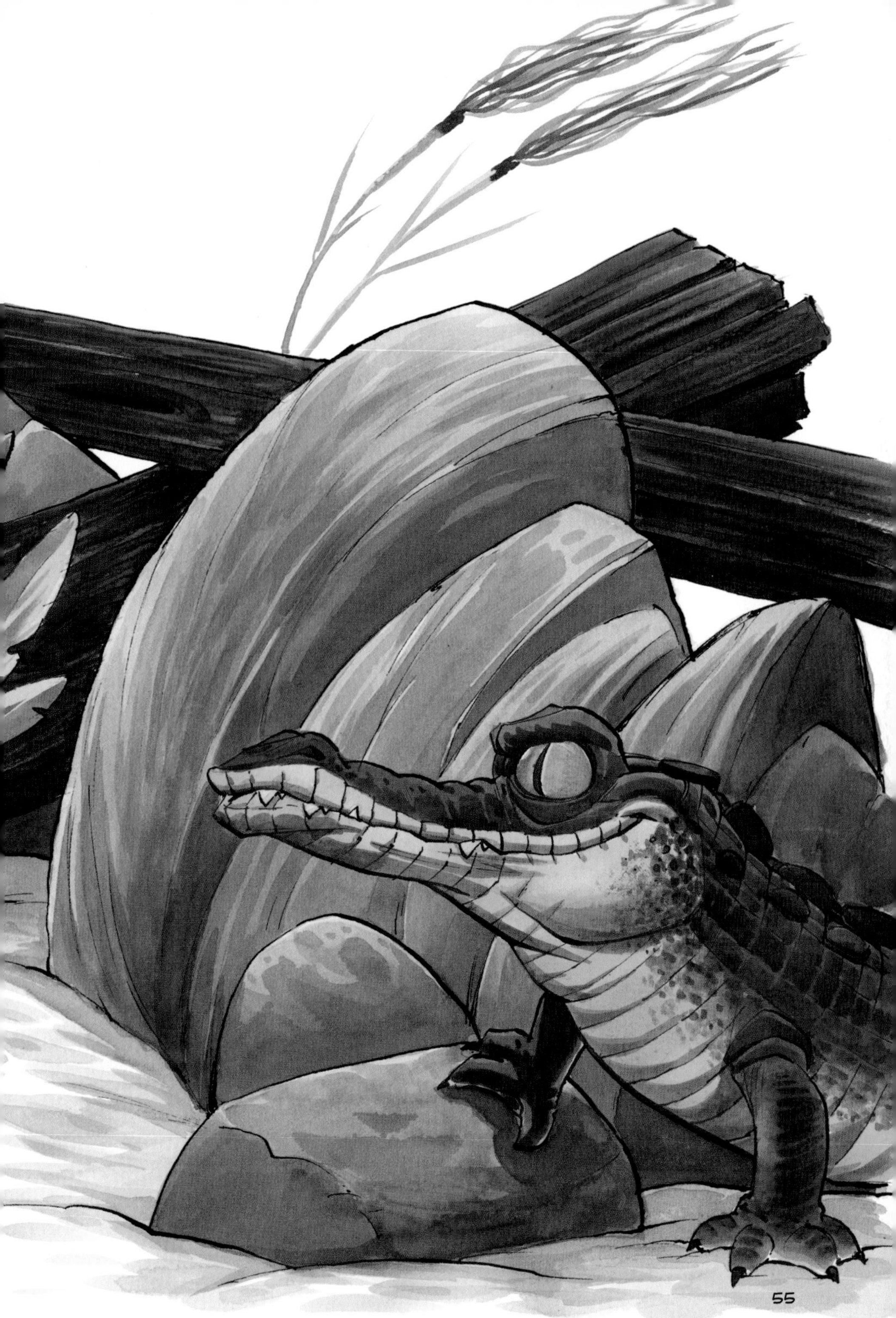

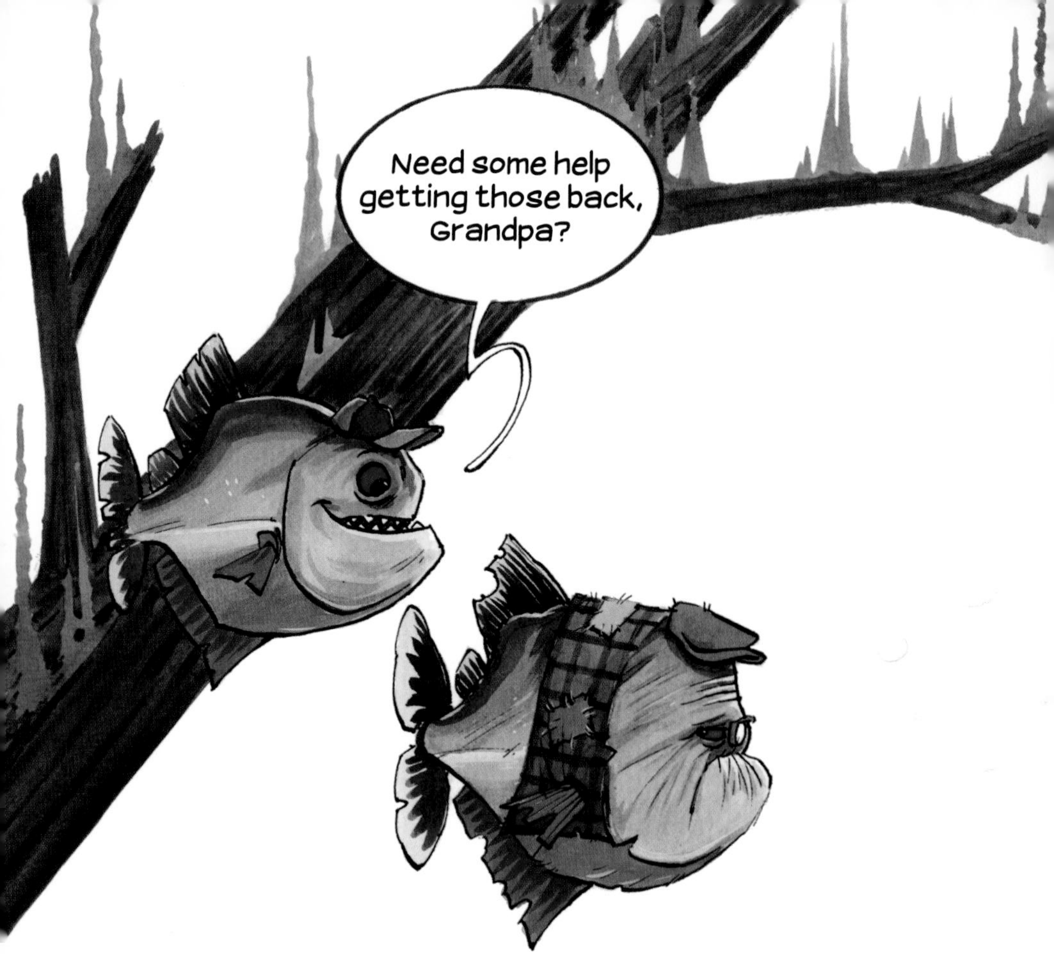
Need some help getting those back, Grandpa?

Piranhas can live for 10 to 15 years.

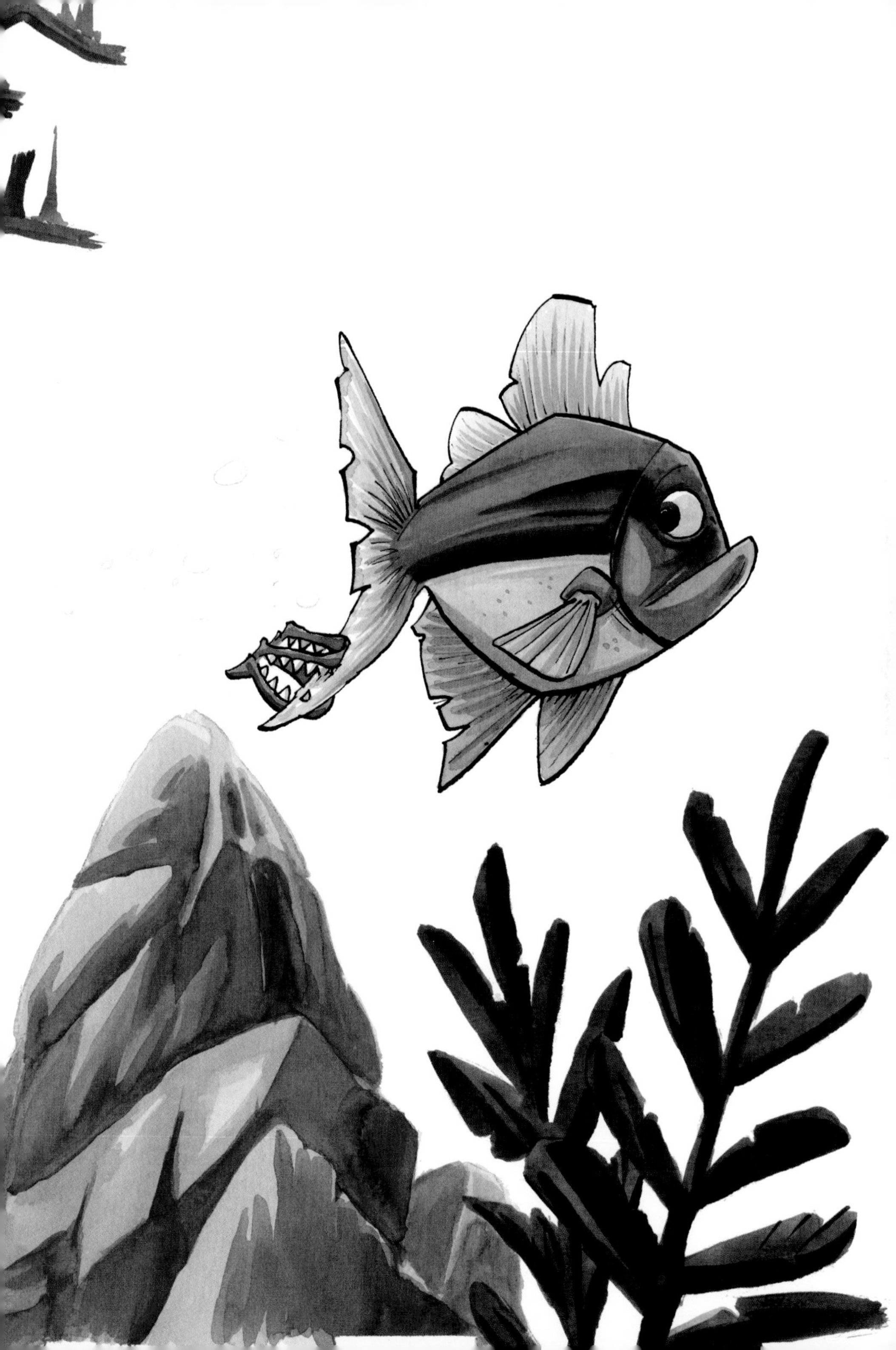

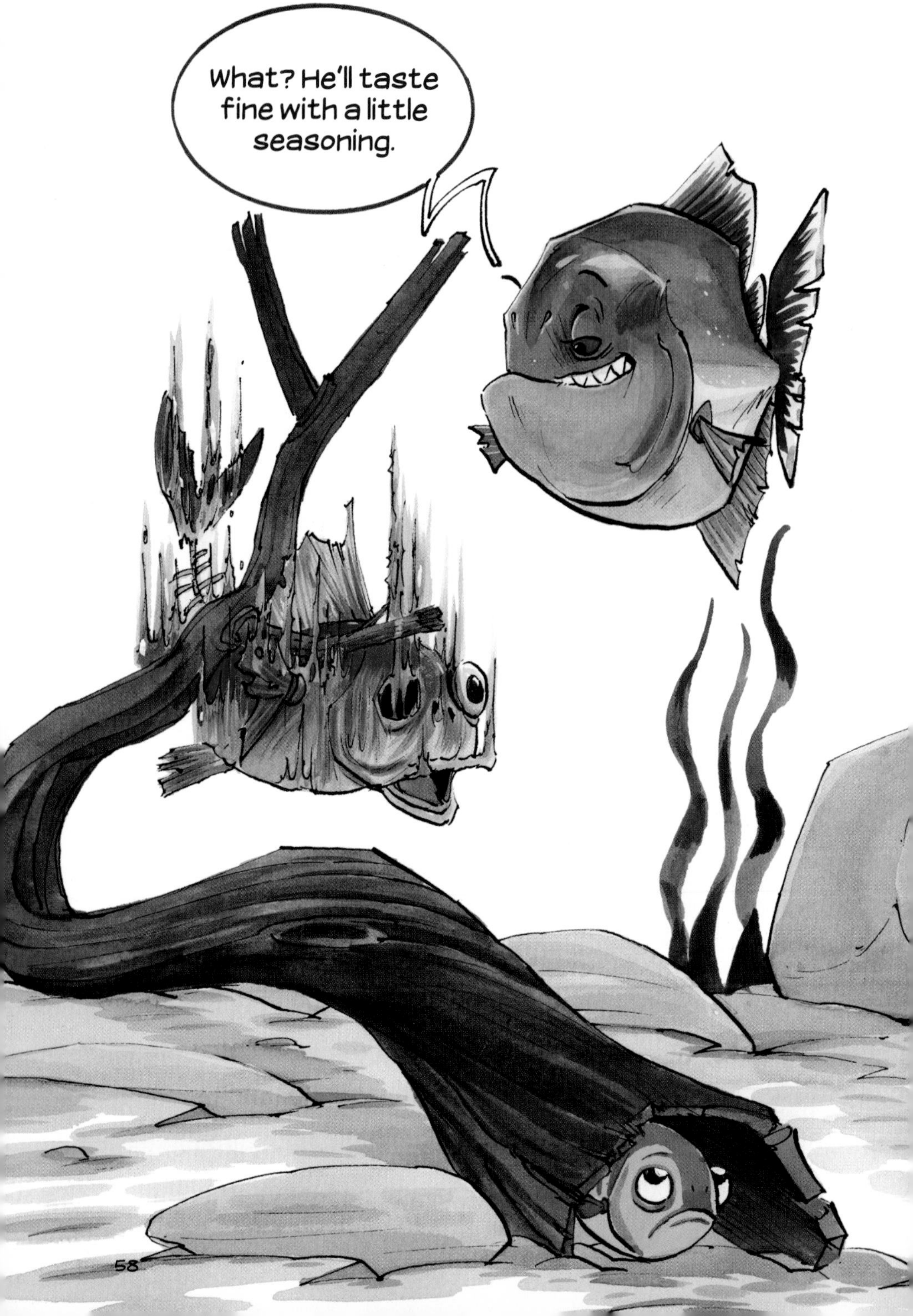
What? He'll taste fine with a little seasoning.

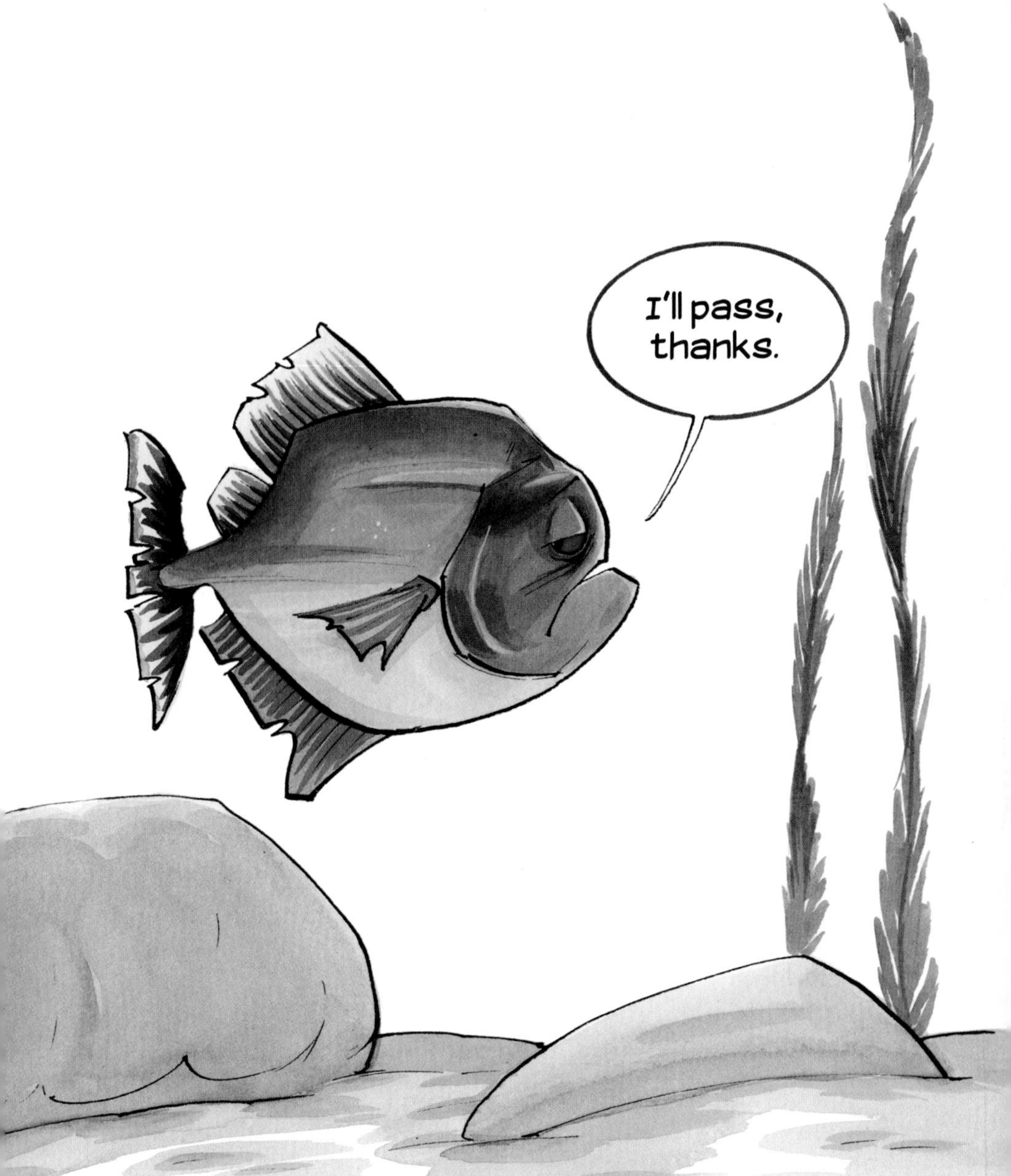
I'll pass, thanks.

They help keep rivers clean.

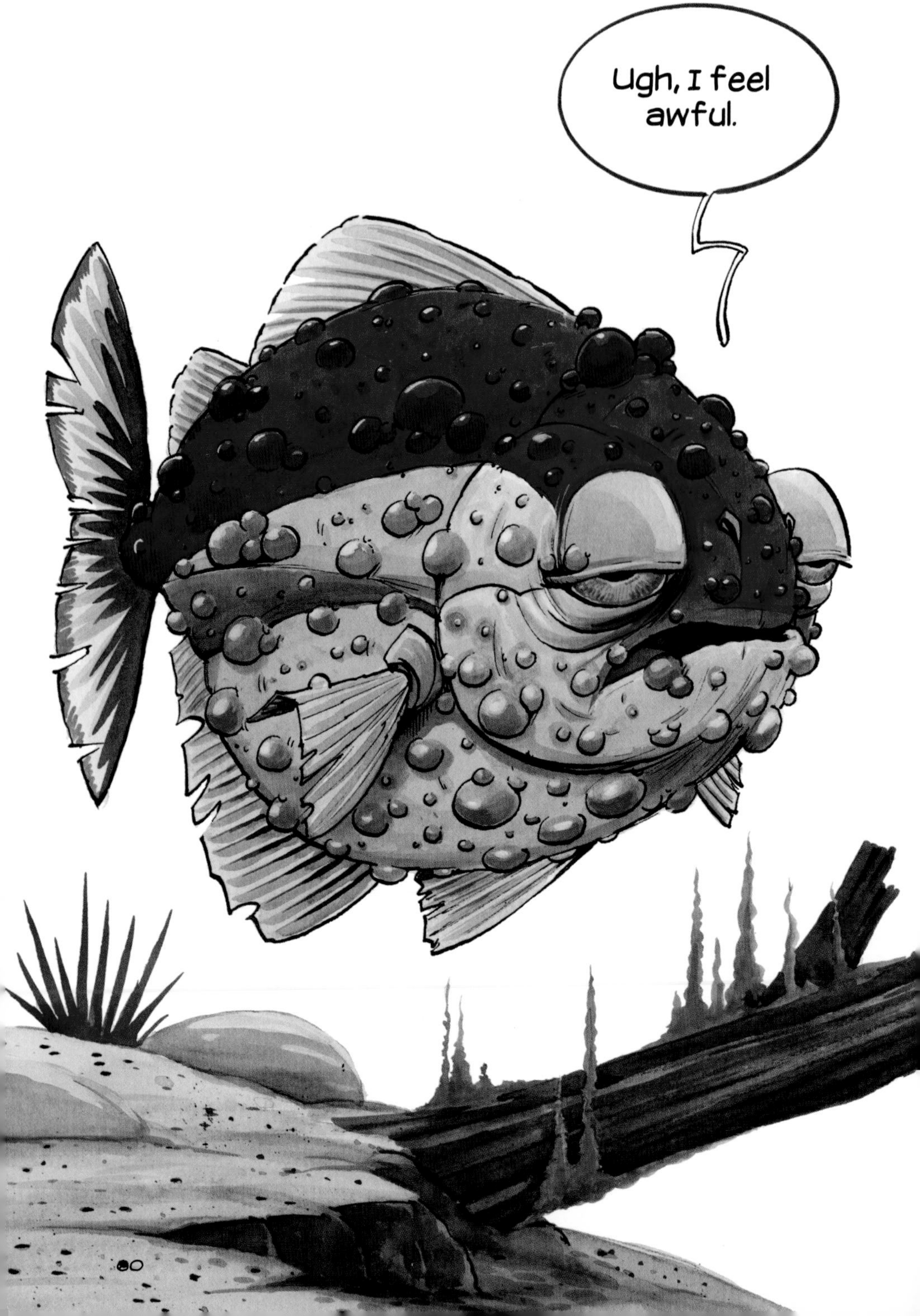
Ugh, I feel awful.

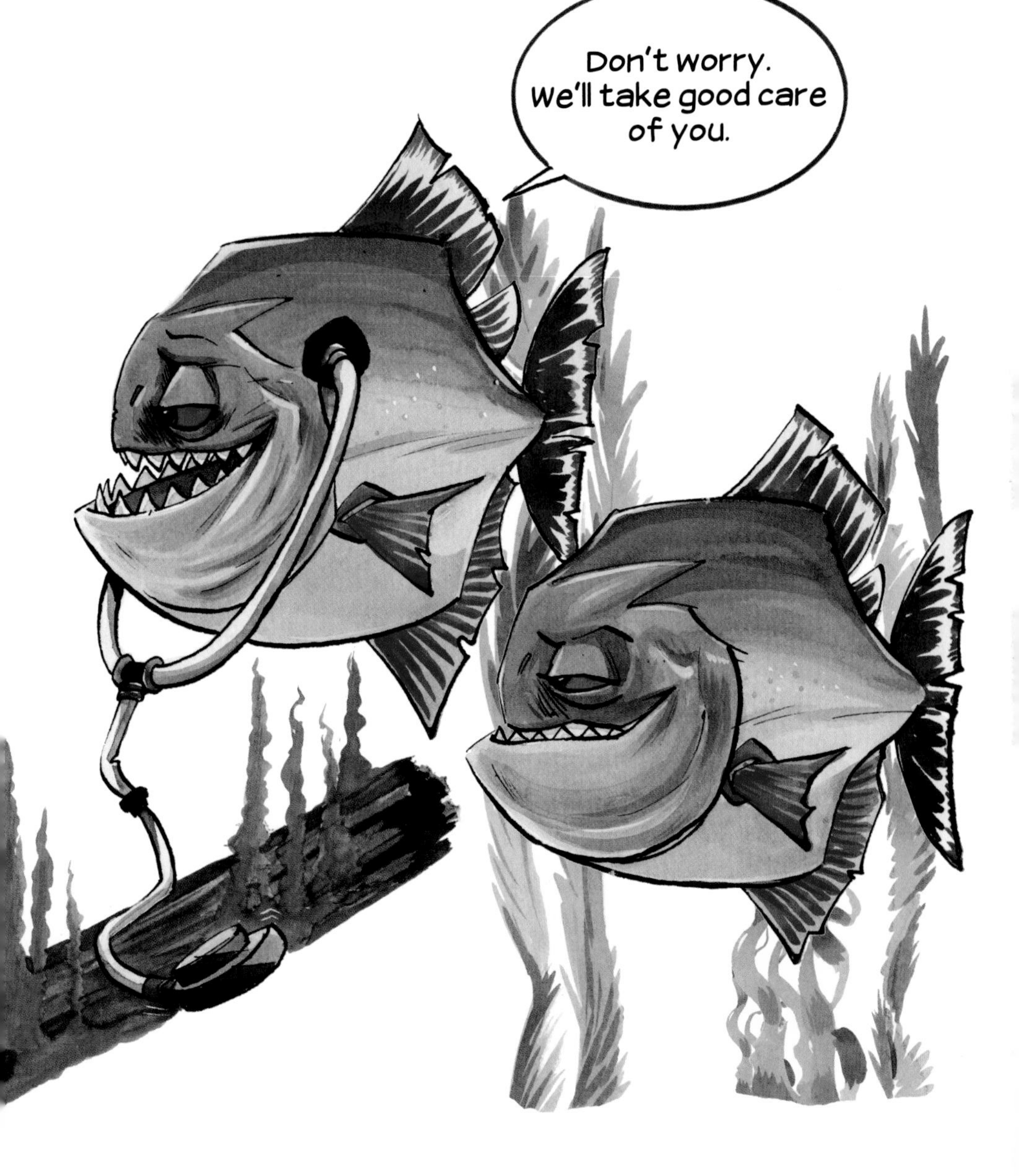
Don't worry.
We'll take good care
of you.

By keeping rivers clean of sick fish, piranhas even control **epidemics**.

Glossary

Ambush a surprise attack

Caiman a type of crocodilian, similar to an alligator, that lives in South and Central America

Cannibal an animal that feeds on its own species

Epidemic the rapid spread of a disease to many individuals of a population in a short time

Mammal a warm-blooded, back-boned animal

Prey an animal hunted and killed by another for food

Reptile a cold-blooded, back-boned animal covered in scales or hard parts, such as a snake, lizard, or crocodile

Shoal a large group of fish swimming together

Soft water water that is free from salt

Species a classification for a group of creatures with common characteristics

Vegetarian a creature that does not eat meat

Index

behaviour 50–51

cannibalism 26–29

diet 14–23, 58–61

eating habits 34–37

habitat 4–5

hunting 38–43, 46–49

life span 56–57

predators 52–55

scavenging 24–25

senses 30–33

shoal 12–13

size 8–9

species 6–7, 44–45

teeth 10–11

Do You Know there are other titles?

Rats

Crows

Crocodiles

Leeches

Chameleons

Toads

Spiders